DIABETIC
COOKBOOK
FOR TEENAGERS

Healthy, Delicious Recipes with Pictures to help Teenagers Manage Diabetes. Includes 30-days Meal Plan

Jane D. Tumlin

All rights reserved. No part of this publication may be reproduced, distributed, or transmitted in any form or by any means, including photocopying, recording, or other electronic or mechanical methods, without the prior written permission of the publisher, except in the case of brief quotations embodied in critical reviews and certain other non-commercial uses permitted by copyright law.

Copyright © Jane D. Tumlin 2023

TABLE OF CONTENTS

INTRODUCTION 7

CHAPTER 1 BASICS OF DIABETES AND HEALTHY EATING 9

    Understanding Diabetes 9

    Understanding Carbohydrates, Proteins and Fats 10

    Eating for a healthy diabetes 11

    Best vegetables and fruits for diabetic patient 13

CHAPTER 2 BREAKFAST RECIPES 17

    Oatmeal with fresh fruit 17

    Egg whites with a side of grilled vegetables 19

    Scrambled tofu with spinach 21

    Greek yoghourt with nuts and seeds 23

    Avocado toast on whole-grain bread 25

    Peanut butter and banana on whole-wheat toast 27

    Low-fat cottage cheese and berries 29

    Steel-cut oatmeal with almond milk 31

    Homemade vegetable omelette 33

    Almond flour pancakes with blueberries 35

    Quinoa porridge with cinnamon 41

    Smoothie with almond milk, spinach, and banana ... 43

    Oat bran muffins with walnuts 45

    Farro with roasted vegetables 48

CHAPTER 3 LUNCH RECIPES 51

    Baked Salmon with Vegetables 51

Grilled Chicken and Mixed Greens Salad 53

Quinoa Bowl with Avocado and Chickpeas 55

Turkey Wraps with Spinach and Hummus 57

Roasted Vegetable and Brown Rice Bowl 59

Baked Sweet Potatoes with Black Beans 61

Vegetable and Bean Soup 63

Turkey and Cheese Sandwich on Whole Wheat Bread 65

Greek Yogurt Parfait with Berries 67

Egg Salad on Whole Wheat Bread 68

Broccoli and Cheddar Omelette 70

Chicken and Vegetable Stir-Fry 72

Lentil and Kale Stew 74

Tuna and White Bean Salad 77

Turkey and Veggie Burger on a Whole Wheat Bun .. 79

CHAPTER 4 DINNER RECIPES 81

Grilled Fish with Sautéed Vegetables 81

Baked Chicken and Spinach Salad 83

Lentil Soup with Brown Rice 85

Roasted Turkey with Sweet Potatoes 87

Spaghetti Squash with Marinara Sauce 89

Grilled Salmon with Roasted Asparagus 91

Quinoa Salad with Shrimp 93

Baked Tilapia with Broccoli 95

Stuffed Peppers with Brown Rice 97

Vegetable Stir Fry 99

Baked Sweet Potato Fries.. 101
Grilled Chicken with Quinoa 103
Chickpea and Butternut Squash Curry 105
Greek Salad with Tuna... 107
Turkey Burger with Lettuce and Tomato 109

CHAPTER 5 SNACKS RECIPES 111

High-fibre crackers with peanut butter 111
Air-popped popcorn.. 112
Greek yoghourt with berries.. 114
Celery sticks with hummus 115
Apple slices with almond butter.................................... 117
Edamame... 118
Nuts and seeds 120
Trail mix with dried fruit.. 122
Cottage cheese with fruit.. 124
Whole-grain toast with avocado.................................... 126
Cucumber slices with tuna... 128
Roasted chickpeas 129
Hard-boiled eggs.. 131
Low-fat string cheese... 132
Protein smoothie with almond milk 134

CHAPTER 6 DESSERT RECIPES 137

Apple slices with cinnamon... 137
Frozen yogurt... 139
Baked pears with cinnamon.. 141
Sugar-free pudding 143

Baked apples with raisins and cinnamon 145

Angel food cake 147

Sugar-free cookies 149

Sugar-free ice cream 151

Sugar-free gelatine 153

Baked oatmeal with dried fruit 155

Sugar-free brownies 157

Baked sweet potatoes with cinnamon 159

Baked bananas with cinnamon 161

Yogurt parfait with fresh fruit 163

Sugar-free smoothies 165

CHAPTER 7 30 DAYS MEAL PLAN 167

CONCLUSION 175

BONUS 177

10 Exercises 177

Daily Routine: 179

Weekly Meal Planner 181

Food Journal 182

Blood Sugar Log Book 183

INTRODUCTION

Steve was diagnosed with Type 2 diabetes about five years ago. He was devastated when he heard the news and did not know what to do. He was scared of the potential complications that could come with diabetes, such as blindness and kidney failure. His doctor suggested that he start an exercise routine and follow a healthy diet to help manage his diabetes.

Steve decided to start researching and found a diabetic cookbook Recipes. He found the recipes in the book to be helpful and was able to make small changes to his diet. After a few months, Steve was able to reduce his sugar level. He was amazed at the results and was excited to share his success with his doctor.

Steve continued to follow the recipes in the cookbook and was able to maintain a healthy diet. He also started to exercise more and was able to keep his sugar levels in check.

Steve was now living a healthier lifestyle thanks to the diabetic cookbook Recipes. He was able to better manage his diabetes and he was feeling much better than before.

He was thankful that the cookbook had helped him make the changes necessary to improve his health.

Cooking for teens with diabetes can be a challenge. In this cookbook, we provide delicious, nutritious recipes that are tailored toward the needs of teenagers living with diabetes. We understand that teenage palates can be finicky and that teens often have their own creative ideas when it comes to food. That is why our recipes are designed to be both delicious and nutritious while still allowing teens to experiment and have fun with their food.

We have included a wide variety of recipes that focus on whole, unprocessed foods, such as fruits, vegetables, lean proteins, and whole grains. We also provide tips for how to modify recipes for diabetics, so that teens can still enjoy their favourite dishes without sacrificing nutrition.

Our cookbook is designed to give teens with diabetes the confidence to explore their culinary creativity and to make healthy decisions about their eating habits. With our recipes and guidance, teens can learn to cook delicious, nutritious meals that are tailored to their diabetes needs.

CHAPTER 1 BASICS OF DIABETES AND HEALTHY EATING

Understanding Diabetes

Diabetes is a chronic condition that occurs when there is an imbalance of the hormones insulin and glucose in the body. Glucose is a type of sugar that is found in the foods we eat and is used by the body for energy. Insulin is a hormone produced by the pancreas that helps the body use and store glucose.

When someone has diabetes, their body either does not produce enough insulin or cannot use the insulin it produces efficiently. This causes the levels of glucose in the blood to rise, leading to hyperglycaemia.

The two main types of diabetes are type 1 and type 2.

Type 1 diabetes: Is an autoimmune disorder in which the body's immune system attacks and destroys the cells in the pancreas that produce insulin. This means that people with type 1 diabetes require insulin injections to maintain normal blood glucose levels.

Type 2 diabetes: Is a metabolic disorder in which the body does not produce enough insulin or does not use the insulin it produces efficiently.

It is typically caused by lifestyle factors such as being overweight or having an unhealthy diet. People with type 2 diabetes may be able to control their condition with diet and exercise, but may also require medication or insulin injections.

People with diabetes should take steps to manage their condition, such as regularly testing their blood glucose levels, eating a healthy diet, getting regular physical activity, and managing stress. It is also important to see a doctor regularly to monitor diabetes and make sure it is being managed properly.

Understanding Carbohydrates, Proteins and Fats

Carbohydrates, proteins, and fats are macronutrients, meaning they are needed in large amounts by the body.

All three of these macronutrients play an important role in diabetes management.

Carbohydrates: Carbohydrates are the body's main source of energy and are found in foods like grains, fruits, vegetables, and dairy products. Eating high-fibre carbohydrates, such as whole grains and no starchy vegetables, can help keep blood sugar levels in check.

People with diabetes should also watch their carbohydrate intake and spread out their carbohydrate servings throughout the day to help maintain steady blood sugar levels.

Proteins: Proteins are essential for building and repairing muscle, and can be found in foods like meat, fish, legumes, and dairy products. Eating proteins with carbohydrates can help slow down the absorption of carbohydrates, which can help prevent blood sugar spikes.

Fats: Fats are an important source of energy and help keep the body warm. They can be found in foods like nuts, seeds, avocados, and oils.

It's important to choose healthy fats, like monounsaturated and polyunsaturated fats, and limit saturated and Trans fats.

Eating for a healthy diabetes

Healthy eating is an important part of managing diabetes, especially for teenagers. Eating healthy meals and snacks can help you control your blood sugar, maintain a healthy weight, and stay energised throughout the day. Here are some basic tips for healthy eating:

1. Choose nutrient-rich foods: Most of your meals should be made up of nutrient-rich foods, such as fruits, vegetables, whole grains, lean proteins, and healthy fats.

These foods are packed with vitamins, minerals, fibre, and phytonutrients that help support your overall health, as well as your diabetes management.

2. Eat plenty of fruits, vegetables, and whole grains: Fruits, vegetables, and whole grains are important sources of nutrients like fibre and vitamins. They can also help you feel full longer and help control your blood sugar. Aim for at least three servings of each per day.

3. Limit processed and sugary foods: Eating too many processed and sugary foods can cause your blood sugar to spike and can contribute to weight gain.

Avoid high-sugar foods like candy, cookies, and cakes, and limit processed foods like frozen dinners, chips, and crackers.

4. Make healthy carb choices: Carbs like bread, cereal, and rice can affect your blood sugar levels. Choose whole-grain carbs like whole wheat bread and brown rice, and limit your intake of refined carbs like white bread and white rice.

5. Choose lean proteins: Protein helps keep you full and can help control your blood sugar. Try to include lean proteins like skinless chicken, fish, and beans in your meals.

6. Monitor your portion sizes: Eating too much of any food can cause your blood sugar to spike.

Try to stick to recommended portion sizes and practice mindful eating by taking your time while eating and not eating until you're full.

7. Exercise regularly: Exercise helps you manage your blood sugar levels and can also help you maintain a healthy weight. Aim for at least 30 minutes of physical activity most days of the week.

8. Drink plenty of water: Staying hydrated helps your body keep your blood sugar steady. Aim for at least 8 cups of water each day.

9. Get adequate sleep: Sleep helps your body regulate your blood sugar levels. Aim for at least 7-8 hours of sleep each night.

10. Have regular check-ups with your doctor: Regular check-ups with your doctor can help make sure your diabetes is under control.

Best vegetables and fruits for diabetic patient

Teenagers with diabetes need a well-balanced and nutritious diet that can help them manage their blood sugar levels. Including a variety of vegetables and fruits in their diet is an essential part of a healthy meal plan. Here are some of the best vegetables and fruits for teenage diabetic patients:

Non-Starchy Vegetables: Non-starchy vegetables are low in carbohydrates and calories and high in fibre, vitamins, and minerals. These vegetables include broccoli, cauliflower, spinach, kale, carrots, cucumber, cabbage, Brussels sprouts, and lettuce. They help to keep blood sugar levels stable and maintain good overall health.

Berries: Berries are low in calories, high in fibre, and packed with vitamins and antioxidants. They help to lower blood sugar levels and reduce inflammation. Berries such as blueberries, strawberries, raspberries, and blackberries are a good option for diabetic teenagers.

Apples: Apples are high in fibre and low in calories, making them a good choice for diabetic teenagers.

The fibre in apples slows down the digestion of carbohydrates, which helps to keep blood sugar levels stable. Apples also contain antioxidants that help to reduce inflammation and improve overall health.

Citrus Fruits: Citrus fruits such as oranges, grapefruits, and lemons are high in vitamin C and fibre. They are also low in calories and carbohydrates, which makes them a good option for diabetic teenagers. Vitamin C in citrus fruits can help to lower blood sugar levels and improve overall health.

Avocado: Avocado is a low-carbohydrate fruit that is high in fibre, healthy fats, and vitamins. It can help to improve insulin sensitivity and reduce the risk of heart disease. Avocado is also a good source of potassium, which can help to regulate blood pressure.

Tomatoes: Tomatoes are low in calories and carbohydrates and high in vitamins and antioxidants. They are also a good source of lycopene, a powerful antioxidant that can help to reduce the risk of heart disease. Tomatoes are a good option for diabetic teenagers as they help to keep blood sugar levels stable.

Sweet Potatoes: Sweet potatoes are a good source of fibre, vitamins, and minerals. They are also low in calories and carbohydrates. The fibre in sweet potatoes helps to slow down the digestion of carbohydrates, which helps to keep blood sugar levels stable.

In conclusion, a well-balanced diet including a variety of vegetables and fruits is essential for teenage diabetic patients.

The above-mentioned fruits and vegetables can help to manage blood sugar levels, reduce inflammation, and improve overall health. However, it is important to consult a doctor or a registered dietician before making any significant changes to a teenager's diet.

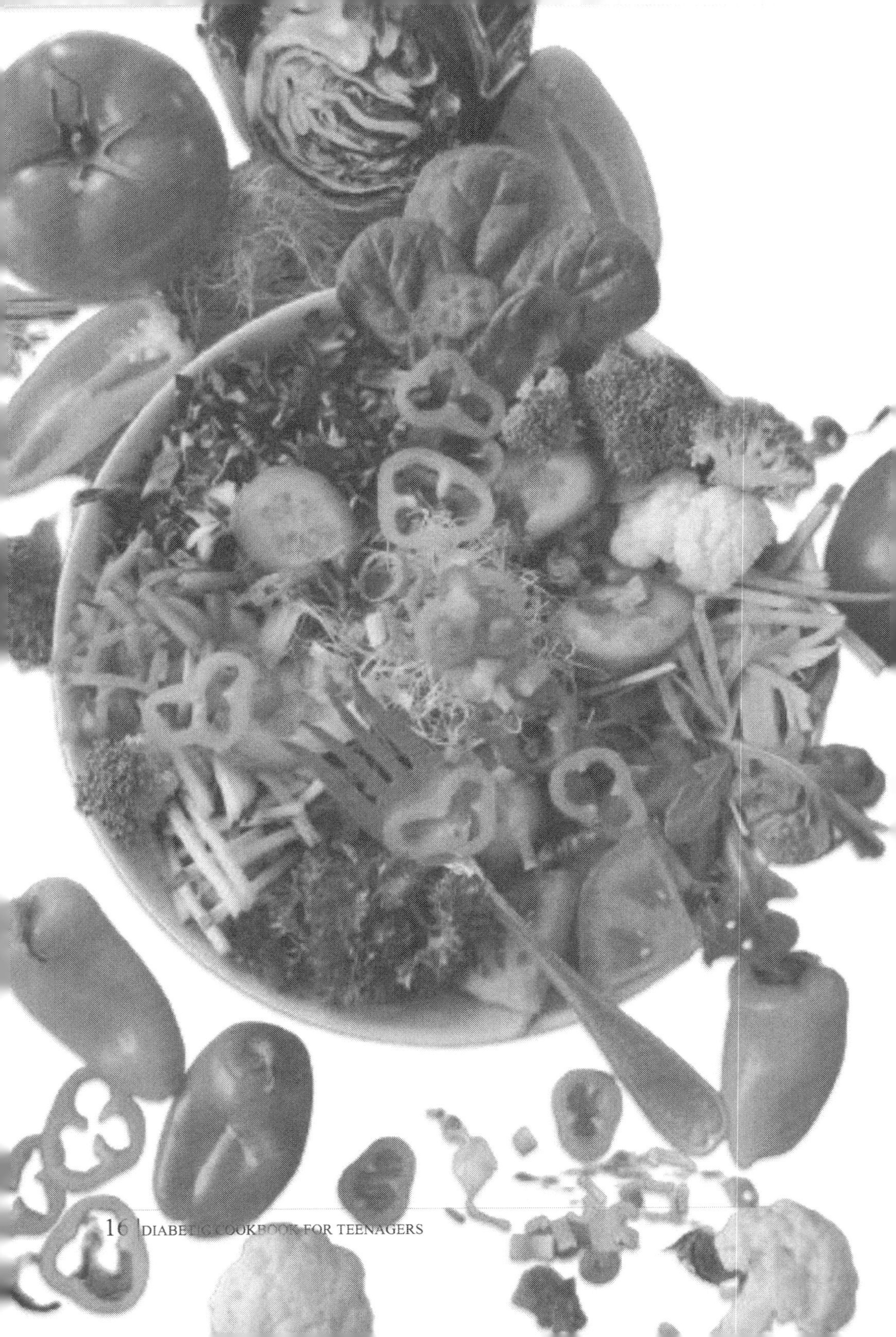

CHAPTER 2 BREAKFAST RECIPES

Oatmeal with fresh fruit

Preparation Time: 5 minutes

Cooking Time: 10 minutes

Servings: 1

Ingredients:

- 1/2 cup rolled oats
- 1 cup unsweetened almond milk
- 1/2 cup mixed fresh fruit (such as berries, chopped apple or banana)
- 1 tablespoon chopped nuts (such as almonds or walnuts)

- 1/2 teaspoon ground cinnamon
- 1/2 teaspoon vanilla extract
- 1 teaspoon honey (optional)

Directions:

> In a medium saucepan, combine the rolled oats and almond milk. Bring to a boil over medium-high heat, stirring frequently.

> Reduce heat to medium-low and simmer for 5 minutes, or until the oats are cooked and the mixture has thickened.

> Add the cinnamon and vanilla extract to the oatmeal and stir to combine.

> Transfer the oatmeal to a serving bowl and top with the fresh fruit and chopped nuts.

> Drizzle with honey, if desired.

> Enjoy your delicious and healthy oatmeal with fresh fruit.

Nutrition Facts (per serving): Calories: 300 Total Fat: 9g Saturated Fat: 1g Cholesterol: 0mg Sodium: 90mg Total Carbohydrate: 47g Dietary Fibre: 8g Sugars: 17g Protein: 9g

Egg whites with a side of grilled vegetables

Preparation time: 10 minutes

Cooking time: 20 minutes

Servings: 2

Ingredients:

- 4 egg whites
- 1 tablespoon olive oil
- 1 small zucchini, sliced
- 1 small yellow squash, sliced
- 1 red bell pepper, sliced
- 1 small red onion, sliced
- 1 teaspoon garlic powder

- 1 teaspoon dried basil
- Salt and black pepper to taste

Directions:

- Preheat your grill to medium heat.
- In a mixing bowl, whisk the egg whites until frothy. Season with salt and black pepper to taste.
- In a large skillet over medium heat, heat the olive oil. Add the zucchini, yellow squash, red bell pepper, and red onion. Sprinkle it with garlic powder and dried basil. Cook for 5-7 minutes, or until the vegetables are tender and lightly charred. Season with salt and black pepper to taste.
- While the vegetables are cooking, place the egg whites in a non-stick skillet over medium heat. Cook for 3-5 minutes, or until the egg whites are set and cooked through.
- Divide the egg whites and grilled vegetables evenly between two plates. Serve immediately.
- Enjoy your delicious and healthy meal.

Nutrition facts (per serving): Calories: 180 Protein: 16g Fat: 9g Carbohydrates: 12g Fibre: 3g Sugar: 7g Sodium: 370mg Cholesterol: 0mg

Scrambled tofu with spinach

Preparation Time: 10 minutes

Cooking time: 10 minutes

Servings: 2

Ingredients:

- 1 block (14oz) of firm tofu
- 1 tablespoon olive oil
- 2 cups of fresh spinach leaves
- 1 teaspoon garlic powder
- 1 teaspoon onion powder
- Salt and black pepper to taste

Directions

- Remove the tofu from the packaging and drain the excess liquid. Wrap the tofu in a clean kitchen towel or paper towels and gently press to remove any remaining moisture.
- In a large skillet over medium heat, heat the olive oil. Crumble the tofu into the skillet and season with garlic powder, onion powder, salt, and black pepper. Cook for 5-7 minutes, or until the tofu is lightly browned and slightly crispy.
- Add the fresh spinach leaves to the skillet and stir until the spinach is wilted and tender, about 2-3 minutes.
- Serve immediately and enjoy!

Nutrition facts (per serving): Calories: 150 Protein: 14g Fat: 9g Carbohydrates: 4g Fibre: 2g Sugar: 1g Sodium: 150mg Cholesterol: 0mg

Greek yoghourt with nuts and seeds

Preparation Time: 5 minutes

Cooking Time: 10 minutes

Servings: 1

Ingredients:

- 1 cup Greek yoghourt
- 1 tablespoon chopped almonds
- 1 tablespoon chopped walnuts
- 1 tablespoon chia seeds
- 1 tablespoon pumpkin seeds
- 1 teaspoon honey (optional)

Directions:

- In a small bowl, mix together the Greek yoghurt and honey (if using) until well combined.
- Top the yoghurt with the chopped almonds, walnuts, chia seeds, and pumpkin seeds.
- Serve immediately and enjoy!

Nutrition Facts (per serving): Calories: 314 Total Fat: 16g Saturated Fat: 2g Cholesterol: 11 mg Sodium: 87 mg Total Carbohydrates: 19g Dietary Fibre: 6g Total Sugars: 8g Protein: 24g

Avocado toast on whole-grain bread

Preparation Time: 5 minutes

Cooking Time: 5 minutes

Servings: 1

Ingredients:

- 1 slice of whole-grain bread
- 1/2 ripe avocado
- 1/4 teaspoon of sea salt
- 1/4 teaspoon of black pepper
- 1/2 teaspoon of lemon juice
- 1/2 small tomato, sliced

- 1/4 small red onion, thinly sliced
- 1/4 cup of arugula
- 1 teaspoon of olive oil

Directions

- Toast the slice of whole-grain bread until golden brown.
- Cut the avocado in half and remove the pit. Scoop out the flesh into a small bowl.
- Add the sea salt, black pepper, and lemon juice to the avocado. Mash with a fork until the mixture is smooth.
- Spread the mashed avocado onto the toasted bread.
- Top with sliced tomatoes, red onion, and arugula.
- Drizzle with olive oil and serve immediately.

Nutrition Facts (per serving): Calories: 280 Total Fat: 18g Saturated Fat: 2.5g Trans Fat: 0g Cholesterol: 0mg Sodium: 400mg Total Carbohydrates: 25g Dietary Fibre: 9g Sugars: 4g Protein: 6g

Peanut butter and banana on whole-wheat toast

Preparation Time: 5 minutes

Cooking Time: 5 minutes

Servings: 1

Ingredients

- 1 slice of whole-wheat bread
- 1 tablespoon of natural peanut butter
- 1/2 medium banana, sliced

Directions

- ➢ Preheat your toaster to your desired setting.
- ➢ While the toaster is heating up, take out your slice of whole-wheat bread and spread 1 tablespoon of natural peanut butter on it.
- ➢ Slice half of a medium banana and lay the slices on top of the peanut butter.
- ➢ Once the toaster is ready, place the slice of bread with peanut butter and banana into the toaster and cook for 1-2 minutes or until the bread is toasted to your liking.
- ➢ Once the toast is done, take it out of the toaster and let it cool for a minute.
- ➢ Cut the toast in half and serve.

Nutrition Facts (per serving): Calories: 260 Carbohydrates: 33g Protein: 9g Fat: 11g Fibre: 6g Sugar: 9g Sodium: 170mg

Low-fat cottage cheese and berries

Preparation Time: 10 minutes

Cooking Time: 10 minutes

Servings: 1

Ingredients

- 1/2 cup low-fat cottage cheese
- 1/2 cup mixed berries (blueberries, strawberries, raspberries)
- 1 tsp. honey (optional)

Directions

➢ Wash the berries and cut the strawberries into small pieces.

➢ In a bowl, add the cottage cheese and mix in the berries.

➢ If desired, add a teaspoon of honey for sweetness.

➢ Serve chilled and enjoy!

Nutrition Facts (per serving): Calories: 120 Protein: 13g Fat: 2g Carbohydrates: 15g Fibre: 4g Sodium: 350mg

Steel-cut oatmeal with almond milk

Preparation Time: 5 minutes

Cooking Time: 30 minutes

Servings: 2

Ingredients:

- 1 cup steel-cut oats
- 2 cups unsweetened almond milk
- 1/4 tsp. salt
- 1 tsp. cinnamon
- 1/4 cup chopped almonds
- 2 tbsp. maple syrup (optional)

Directions:

- In a medium-sized pot, bring 4 cups of water to a boil.
- Add the steel-cut oats and salt to the boiling water, stirring occasionally.
- Reduce the heat to low and let the oats simmer for 20-25 minutes, or until the oats have absorbed most of the water and have a creamy texture.
- Add the almond milk and cinnamon to the pot and stir well.
- Cook the oats on low heat for another 5-10 minutes until they reach the desired consistency.
- Divide the oatmeal into two bowls and top with chopped almonds and maple syrup (if desired).
- Serve hot and enjoy!

Nutrition Facts (per serving): Calories: 285 Protein: 11g Fat: 9g Carbohydrates: 43g Fibre: 8g Sodium: 310mg

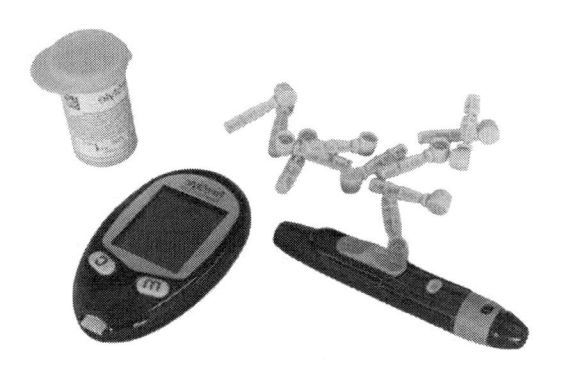

Homemade vegetable omelette

Preparation Time: 10 minutes

Cooking Time: 20 minutes

Servings: 2

Ingredients

- 4 eggs
- 1/4 cup diced red bell pepper
- 1/4 cup diced onion
- 1/4 cup sliced mushrooms
- 1/4 cup chopped spinach
- 1/4 cup shredded cheddar cheese
- 1 tablespoon olive oil
- Salt and pepper to taste

Directions

- Heat the olive oil in a non-stick frying pan over medium heat.
- Add the diced onions and cook until they are soft and translucent, about 2-3 minutes.
- Add the sliced mushrooms and diced red bell pepper to the pan and cook until they are tender, about 3-4 minutes.
- Add the chopped spinach to the pan and cook until it is wilted, about 1-2 minutes.
- Remove the vegetables from the pan and set them aside.
- Crack the eggs into a mixing bowl and whisk them together until they are frothy.
- Pour the eggs into the pan and let them cook until the edges start to set, about 2-3 minutes.
- Use a spatula to gently lift the edges of the omelette and let the uncooked egg run underneath.
- Once the eggs are mostly set, sprinkle the shredded cheddar cheese over one side of the omelette.
- Add the cooked vegetables to the same side of the omelette.
- Use the spatula to fold the other side of the omelette over the vegetables and cheese.
- Let the omelette cook for another minute or so, until the cheese is melted and the eggs are fully cooked.

- ➢ Slide the omelette onto a plate and season with salt and pepper to taste.
- ➢ Enjoy your delicious and nutritious Homemade Vegetable Omelette!

Nutrition Facts (per serving): Calories: 305 Total Fat: 21g Saturated Fat: 7g Cholesterol: 387 mg Sodium: 350mg Total Carbohydrates: 7g Dietary Fibre: 1g Sugar: 3g Protein: 21g

Almond flour pancakes with blueberries

Preparation Time: 10 minutes

Cooking Time: 15 minutes

Servings: 4

Ingredients:

- 2 cups almond flour
- 2 teaspoons baking powder
- 1/4 teaspoon salt
- 1/4 cup unsweetened almond milk
- 2 tablespoons honey
- 3 eggs
- 1 teaspoon vanilla extract
- 1 cup fresh blueberries
- Cooking spray

Directions

- In a large mixing bowl, whisk together the almond flour, baking powder, and salt until well combined.
- In a separate bowl, beat the eggs until frothy, and then add the almond milk, honey, and vanilla extract. Mix until well combined.
- Add the wet ingredients to the dry ingredients and stir until the batter is smooth.
- Gently fold in the blueberries.
- Heat a non-stick skillet or griddle over medium heat and lightly spray with cooking spray.
- Using a 1/4 cup measuring cup, pour the batter onto the skillet or griddle.
- Cook until the edges are set and the surface is bubbly, then flip the pancake over and cook for an additional 1-2 minutes, or until golden brown.
- Repeat with the remaining batter, spraying the skillet with cooking spray between each batch.
- Serve the pancakes warm, topped with additional blueberries if desired.
- Enjoy your delicious and nutritious almond flour pancakes with blueberries!

Nutrition Facts (per serving): Calories: 273 Total Fat: 22g Saturated Fat: 2g Cholesterol: 124 mg Sodium: 378 mg Total Carbohydrates: 15g Dietary Fibre: 4g Sugars: 8g Protein: 10g

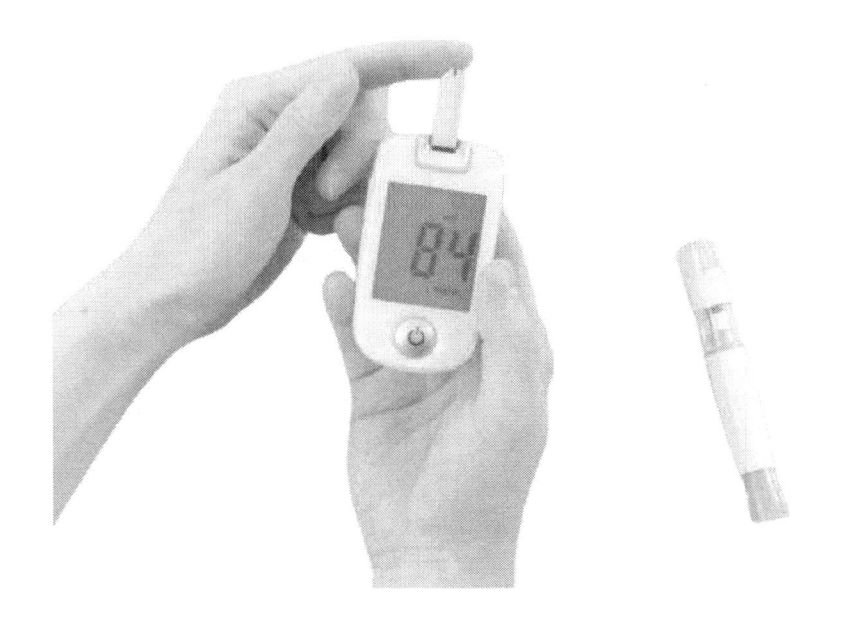

Ezekiel toast with peanut butter

Preparation Time: 5 minutes

Cooking Time: 5 minutes

Servings: 1

Ingredients:

- 1 slice Ezekiel bread
- 1 tablespoon natural peanut butter
- 1 teaspoon honey
- 1/2 banana, sliced
- Pinch of cinnamon (optional)

Directions

- ➤ Preheat the toaster oven to 350°F (175°C).
- ➤ Toast the Ezekiel bread until it is golden brown and crispy.
- ➤ While the bread is toasting, mix the peanut butter and honey in a small bowl until well combined.
- ➤ Once the bread is toasted, spread the peanut butter mixture evenly on top of the slice of bread.
- ➤ Top the peanut butter with the sliced banana and sprinkle with a pinch of cinnamon, if desired.
- ➤ Serve and enjoy!

Nutrition Facts (per serving): Calories: 259 Total Fat: 9.6g Saturated Fat: 1.8g Cholesterol: 0mg Sodium: 180mg Total Carbohydrates: 36.7g Dietary Fibre: 6.9g Total Sugars: 13.8g Protein: 12g

Quinoa porridge with cinnamon

Preparation Time: 5 minutes

Cooking Time: 20 minutes

Servings: 1

Ingredients:

- 1/4 cup uncooked quinoa, rinsed and drained
- 1/2 cup unsweetened almond milk
- 1/2 cup water
- 1/2 teaspoon cinnamon
- 1/4 teaspoon vanilla extract
- 1 tablespoon chopped walnuts
- 1/4 cup fresh blueberries

Directions

- Rinse and drain the quinoa in a fine mesh strainer.
- In a medium saucepan, combine the quinoa, almond milk, water, cinnamon, and vanilla extract. Stir to combine.
- Bring the mixture to a boil over high heat, and then reduce the heat to low and simmer for 15-20 minutes, stirring occasionally, until the quinoa is tender and the liquid has been absorbed.
- Divide the porridge into a bowl and top with chopped walnuts and fresh blueberries.
- Serve and enjoy!

Nutrition Facts (per serving): Calories: 230 Total Fat: 9g Saturated Fat: 0.8g Cholesterol: 0mg Sodium: 88 mg Total Carbohydrates: 32g Dietary Fibre: 6g Total Sugars: 3.7g Protein: 9g

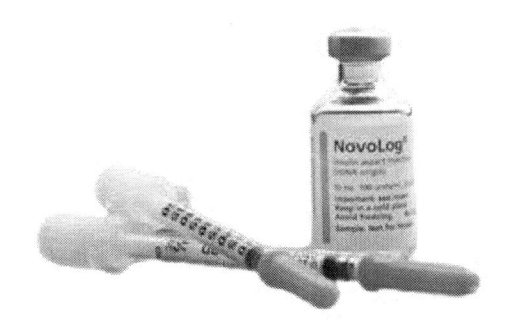

Oat bran muffins with walnuts

Preparation Time: 15 minutes

Cooking Time: 35 minutes

Servings: 12 muffins

Ingredients

- 1 cup oat bran
- 1/2 cup whole wheat flour
- 1/4 cup ground flaxseed
- 1/4 cup chopped walnuts
- 2 teaspoons baking powder
- 1/2 teaspoon baking soda
- 1/4 teaspoon salt
- 1/2 cup unsweetened applesauce

- 1/4 cup pure maple syrup
- 1/4 cup unsweetened almond milk
- 2 tablespoons canola oil
- 2 large eggs
- 1 teaspoon pure vanilla extract

Directions:

- Preheat the oven to 375°F (190°C). Line a 12-cup muffin tin with paper liners or spray with non-stick cooking spray.
- In a large mixing bowl, whisk together the oat bran, whole wheat flour, ground flaxseed, chopped walnuts, baking powder, baking soda, and salt.
- In another mixing bowl, whisk together the applesauce, maple syrup, almond milk, canola oil, eggs, and vanilla extract.
- Add the wet ingredients to the dry ingredients and stir until just combined. Do not over mix the batter.
- Divide the batter evenly among the prepared muffin cups.
- Bake the muffins for 18-20 minutes, or until a toothpick inserted into the centre comes out clean.
- Remove the muffins from the oven and let cool for a few minutes before transferring them to a wire rack to cool completely.

Nutrition Facts (per muffin): Calories: 116 Total Fat: 5.5g Saturated Fat: 0.6g Cholesterol: 27 mg Sodium: 145 mg Total Carbohydrates: 14g Dietary Fibre: 3g Total Sugars: 5g Protein: 4g

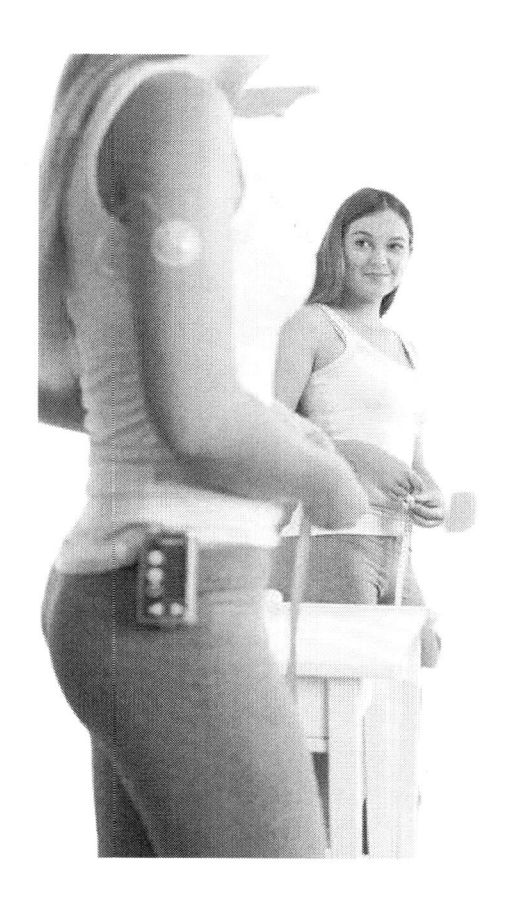

Farro with roasted vegetables

Preparation Time: 15 minutes

Cooking Time: 40 minutes

Servings: 4

Ingredients:

- 1 cup uncooked farro
- 2 cups low-sodium chicken or vegetable broth
- 2 cups mixed vegetables (such as bell peppers, zucchini, and eggplant), chopped into bite-sized pieces
- 1 red onion, chopped into bite-sized pieces
- 3 cloves garlic, minced
- 2 tablespoons olive oil

- Salt and black pepper, to taste
- 1 tablespoon balsamic vinegar
- 2 tablespoons chopped fresh parsley

Directions:

- Preheat the oven to 400°F (200°C).
- In a medium saucepan, bring the farro and chicken or vegetable broth to a boil. Reduce heat, cover, and simmer for 30-35 minutes, or until the farro is tender and the broth is absorbed.
- While the farro is cooking, spread the mixed vegetables and red onion on a baking sheet. Drizzle with olive oil and sprinkle with salt and black pepper.
- Roast in the preheated oven for 20-25 minutes, or until the vegetables are tender and slightly caramelised.
- In a large bowl, whisk together balsamic vinegar, minced garlic, salt, and black pepper.
- Add the cooked farro and roasted vegetables to the bowl, and toss to combine.
- Serve warm, garnished with chopped parsley.

Nutrition facts (per serving): Calories: 360 Total Fat: 10g Saturated Fat: 1g Cholesterol: 0mg Sodium: 250mg Total Carbohydrates: 58g Dietary Fibre: 10g Sugars: 8g Protein: 12g

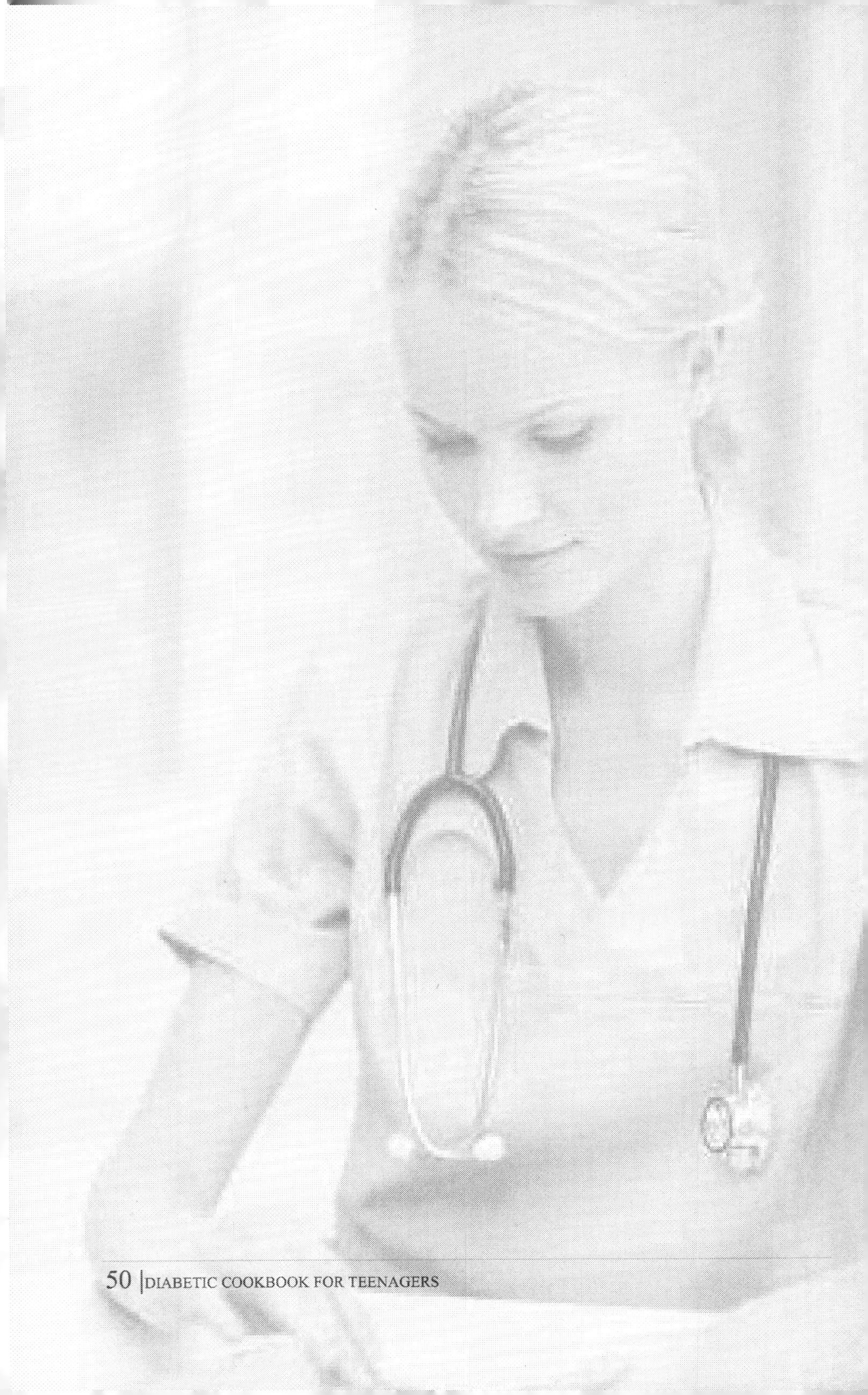

CHAPTER 3 LUNCH RECIPES
Baked Salmon with Vegetables

Preparation Time: 15 minutes

Cooking Time: 35 minutes

Servings: 4

Ingredients:

- 4 salmon fillets
- 2 tablespoons olive oil
- 1 teaspoon garlic powder
- 1 teaspoon onion powder
- 1 teaspoon salt

- 1 teaspoon black pepper
- 1/2 teaspoon paprika
- 1 teaspoon dried oregano
- 2 cups of assorted vegetables (such as bell peppers, carrots, onion, and mushrooms)

Directions:

> Preheat the oven to 375 degrees F (190 degrees C).
> Line a baking sheet with parchment paper.
> Place salmon fillets on the prepared baking sheet and drizzle with olive oil.
> In a small bowl, mix together garlic powder, onion powder, salt, black pepper, paprika, and oregano.
> Sprinkle the spice mixture over the salmon fillets.
> Place the vegetables around the salmon and drizzle with the remaining olive oil.
> Bake in a preheated oven for 25-30 minutes, or until salmon is cooked through and vegetables are tender.

Nutrition Facts (per serving): 1 salmon fillet with 1/2 cup of vegetables Calories: 250 Total Fat: 11g Saturated Fat: 2g Cholesterol: 65 mg Sodium: 500mg Carbohydrates: 10g Fibre: 3g Protein: 30g

Grilled Chicken and Mixed Greens Salad

Preparation Time: 10 minutes

Cooking Time: 15 Minutes

Servings: 2

Ingredients:

- 2 boneless skinless chicken breasts
- 2 tablespoons olive oil
- Salt and pepper to taste
- 2 cups mixed greens
- 1/2 cup cherry tomatoes, halved
- 1/2 cup cucumber, diced
- 1/4 cup red onion, diced
- 2 tablespoons balsamic vinaigrette

Directions:

- Preheat an outdoor grill or grill pan over medium-high heat.
- Brush the chicken breasts with the olive oil, and season with salt and pepper.
- Grill the chicken for 6-8 minutes per side, or until cooked through.
- While the chicken is cooking, assemble the salad in a large bowl.
- Add the mixed greens, tomatoes, cucumber, and red onion.
- Once the chicken is cooked, let it rest for 5 minutes, then slice into strips.
- Add the chicken slices to the salad, and drizzle with the balsamic vinaigrette.
- Toss to combine, and serve.

Nutrition Facts (per serving): Calories: 259 Protein: 28g Carbs: 7g Fat: 14g Fibre: 2g Sugar: 2g

Quinoa Bowl with Avocado and Chickpeas

Preparation Time: 10 minutes

Cooking Time: 15 minutes

Servings: 2

Ingredients:

- 1 cup cooked quinoa
- 1/2 cup cooked chickpeas
- 1/2 diced avocado
- 1/4 cup diced tomatoes
- 1/4 cup diced cucumber
- 1/4 cup diced red onion
- 1 tablespoon olive oil
- 2 tablespoons lemon juice

- 1 teaspoon garlic powder
- Salt and pepper to taste

Directions:

> In a large bowl, combine the cooked quinoa, chickpeas, avocado, tomatoes, cucumber, and red onion.

> In a separate bowl, whisk together the olive oil, lemon juice, garlic powder, salt, and pepper.

> Pour the dressing over the quinoa bowl and mix everything together.

> Divide the quinoa bowl into two servings and enjoy!

Nutrition Facts (per serving): Calories: 300 Fat: 14g

Carbohydrates: 38g Protein: 8g Fibre: 8g Sugar: 4g Sodium: 180mg

Turkey Wraps with Spinach and Hummus

Preparation Time: 10 minutes

Cooking Time: 10 minutes

Servings: 4

Ingredients

- 4 (10 inch) whole wheat tortillas
- 8 ounces thinly sliced deli turkey
- 4 cups fresh spinach leaves
- 1/2 cup Hummus
- Salt and pepper (to taste)

Directions:

- Preheat a large skillet over medium-high heat.
- Place the tortillas in the preheated skillet, and warm each side for about 30 seconds.
- Place the warmed tortillas on a plate or cutting board.
- Divide the turkey slices, spinach leaves, and hummus among the four tortillas.
- Sprinkle it with salt and pepper, to taste.
- Roll up the tortillas, tucking in the sides to keep the filling inside.
- Serve immediately.

Nutrition Facts (per serving): Calories: 183 Protein: 15g Carbohydrates: 25g Fat: 4g Fibre: 6g Sodium: 503m

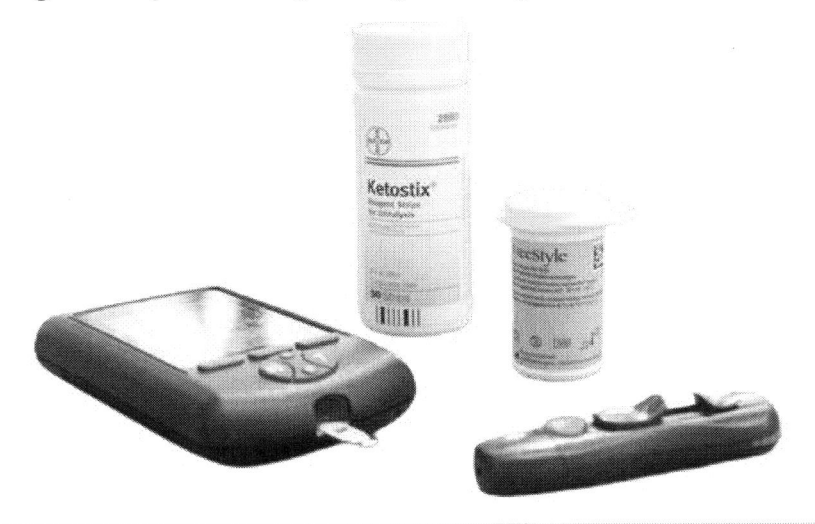

Roasted Vegetable and Brown Rice Bowl

Preparation Time: 15 minutes

Cooking Time: 45 minutes

Servings: 4

Ingredient:

- 2 cups cooked brown rice
- 2 tablespoons olive oil
- 2 cups assorted vegetables (such as cauliflower, bell peppers, zucchini, and mushrooms)
- 2 cloves garlic, minced
- Salt and pepper to taste
- 2 tablespoons chopped parsley

Direction:

- Preheat the oven to 375 degrees F.
- In a large bowl, combine the cooked brown rice with the olive oil, vegetables, garlic, salt, and pepper.
- Spread the mixture evenly on a baking sheet and roast in the preheated oven for 25 minutes.
- Remove from the oven and sprinkle the chopped parsley on top.
- Serve warm.

Nutrition Facts (per serving): Calories: 167 Carbs: 25 g Fat: 7 g Protein: 3 g Fibre: 3 g Sugar: 2 g Sodium: 4 mg

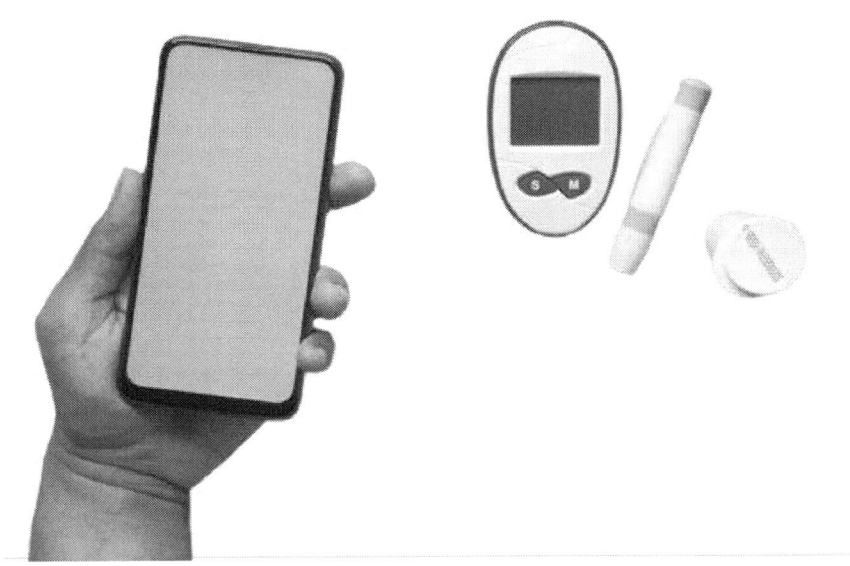

Baked Sweet Potatoes with Black Beans

Preparation Time: 45 minutes

Cooking Time: 45 minutes

Servings: 2

Ingredients:

- 2 sweet potatoes
- 1/4 cup black beans
- 1 tablespoon olive oil
- 1/4 teaspoon chilli powder
- 1/4 teaspoon garlic powder
- 1/4 teaspoon smoked paprika
- 1/4 teaspoon cumin

- salt and pepper, to taste

Directions:

> Preheat the oven to 400 degrees F.
> Wash and scrub the sweet potatoes, and then pierce them a few times with a fork.
> Place the sweet potatoes on a baking sheet and bake for 30 minutes, or until they're fork-tender.
> Heat a small skillet over medium heat and add the olive oil.
> Add the black beans, chilli powder, garlic powder, smoked paprika, and cumin to the skillet and stir until the beans are heated through.
> Once the sweet potatoes are done baking, cut them in half and top with the black bean mixture.
> Add salt and pepper, to taste.

Nutrition Facts (per serving): Calories: 238 Fat: 6.8 g Carbohydrates: 40.4 g Protein: 6.4 g Fibre: 7.2 g Sugar: 7.3 g

Vegetable and Bean Soup

Preparation Time: 20 minutes

Cooking Time: 45 minutes

Servings: 4

Ingredients:

- 2 tablespoons of olive oil
- 1 onion, chopped
- 1 celery rib, chopped
- 1 large carrot, chopped
- 2 cloves of garlic, minced

- 1 quart of vegetable stock
- 2 cups of cooked beans (any kind)
- 2 cups of chopped vegetables (such as zucchini, peppers, and mushrooms)
- 2 tablespoons of fresh herbs (such as thyme, oregano, and parsley)
- Salt and pepper to taste

Directions:

- Heat the olive oil in a large pot over medium heat.
- Add the onion, celery, and carrot and cook until softened, about 5 minutes.
- Add the garlic and cook for 1 minute.
- Add the vegetable stock and bring to a boil.
- Add the beans, vegetables, and herbs. Simmer for 15 minutes.
- Season with salt and pepper to taste.
- Serve hot.

Nutrition Facts (per serving): Calories: 150 Fat: 4.5 g

Carbohydrates: 23 g Protein: 8 g Fibre: 8 g Sodium: 270 mg

Turkey and Cheese Sandwich on Whole Wheat Bread

Preparation Time: 15 minutes

Cooking Time: 15 minutes

Servings: 1

Ingredients:

- 2 slices of whole wheat bread
- 2 slices of turkey
- 2 slices of cheese
- 1 teaspoon of butter

Directions:

- Take two slices of whole wheat bread and spread butter on each slice.
- Place two slices of turkey and two slices of cheese on one slice of bread.
- Place the second slice of bread on top.
- Heat a skillet or griddle over medium heat.
- Place the sandwich in the skillet and cook for 2-3 minutes on each side, or until the cheese is melted and the bread is golden brown and crispy.
- Cut the sandwich in half and enjoy.

Nutrition Facts (per serving): Calories: 435 Fat: 16g Carbohydrates: 43g Protein: 28g Sodium: 732mg Cholesterol: 45mg

Greek Yogurt Parfait with Berries

Preparation Time: 10 minutes

Cooking Time: 0 minutes

Servings: 1

Ingredients:

- 1/2 cup plain Greek yoghourt
- 1/2 cup fresh or frozen berries of your choice
- 1 tablespoon honey or other sweetener
- 1 tablespoon chopped walnuts

Directions:

- In a bowl, combine the yogurt, berries, honey, and walnuts.
- Layer the mixture into a parfait glass.
- Enjoy!

Nutrition Facts (per serving): Calories: 214 Fat: 10g Carbohydrates: 21g Protein: 11g Sugar: 16g Fibre: 3g

Egg Salad on Whole Wheat Bread

Preparation Time: 10 minutes

Cooking Time: 0 minutes

Serves: 1

Ingredients:

- 2 hard-boiled eggs, peeled and chopped
- 1 tablespoon light mayonnaise
- 1 tablespoon Dijon mustard
- 1 teaspoon freshly squeezed lemon juice
- 2 slices whole wheat bread
- Salt and freshly ground black pepper, to taste

Directions:

- In a bowl, combine the eggs, mayonnaise, mustard and lemon juice. Season with salt and pepper.
- Toast the bread and spread the egg salad over the slices.
- Serve and enjoy!

Nutrition Facts (per serving): Calories: 260, Fat: 13.5g, Saturated fat: 2.5g, Cholesterol: 186mg, Sodium: 305mg, Carbohydrates: 21.9g, Fibre: 4.6g, Protein: 13.8g.

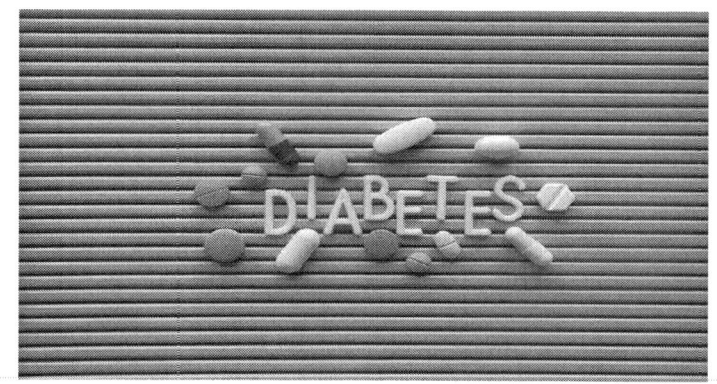

Broccoli and Cheddar Omelette

Preparation Time: 10 minutes

Cooking Time: 10 minutes

Servings: 2

Ingredients:

- 2 eggs
- 1/2 cup broccoli, finely chopped
- 1/3 cup cheddar cheese, shredded
- 2 tablespoons vegetable oil
- Salt and pepper to taste

Directions:

- Heat the oil in a large non-stick skillet over medium-high heat.
- Add the broccoli to the pan and cook for about 5 minutes, stirring occasionally, until the broccoli is tender.
- In a small bowl, whisk together the eggs, salt, and pepper.
- Pour the egg mixture into the pan and cook for about 2 minutes, stirring occasionally, until the eggs begin to set.
- Sprinkle the cheddar cheese over the omelette and cook for another 2 minutes, until the eggs are cooked through.
- Slide the omelette onto a plate and serve.

Nutrition Facts (per serving): 1 omelette Calories: 230

Fat: 16g Carbohydrates: 4g Protein: 16g Sodium: 220mg Fibre: 2g

Chicken and Vegetable Stir-Fry

Preparation Time: 10 minutes

Cooking Time: 15 minutes

Servings: 4

Ingredients:

- 2 tablespoons vegetable oil
- 2 boneless skinless chicken breasts cut into cubes
- 1 onion, diced
- 2 cloves garlic, minced
- 2 cups broccoli florets
- 2 cups diced bell peppers

- 1 cup sliced mushrooms
- 2 tablespoons low sodium soy sauce
- Salt and pepper to taste

Directions:

- Heat the oil in a large skillet over medium-high heat.
- Add the chicken cubes and cook until lightly browned, about 3-4 minutes.
- Add the onion, garlic, broccoli, bell peppers, and mushrooms. Cook, stirring often, until the vegetables are tender, about 5-6 minutes.
- Stir in the soy sauce and season with salt and pepper to taste.
- Cook for an additional 2-3 minutes until the chicken is cooked through.
- Serve over cooked rice or noodles.

Nutrition Facts (per serving): 1/4 of recipe Calories: 256 Total Fat: 9.3 g Saturated Fat: 1.5 g Cholesterol: 43 mg Sodium: 471 mg Carbohydrates: 16.7 g Fibre: 4.7 g Sugar: 4.3 g Protein: 24.3 g

Lentil and Kale Stew

Preparation Time: 10 minutes

Cooking Time: 45 minutes

Servings: 4

Ingredients:

- 1 tablespoon olive oil
- 1 onion, diced
- 2 cloves garlic, minced
- 1 teaspoon ground cumin
- 1 teaspoon ground coriander

- 1 teaspoon paprika
- ½ teaspoon ground turmeric
- 1 cup green lentils
- 1 large potato, peeled and diced
- 4 cups vegetable broth
- 2 cups kale, stemmed and chopped
- 1 teaspoon sea salt
- 1 teaspoon freshly ground black pepper

Directions:

- Heat the olive oil in a large pot over medium heat.
- Add the onion and garlic and sauté for 3-5 minutes, stirring occasionally, until the onion is softened and lightly golden.
- Add the cumin, coriander, paprika, and turmeric and cook for 1 minute, stirring constantly.
- Add the lentils, potato, and vegetable broth and bring to a boil.
- Reduce the heat to low, cover, and simmer for 20 minutes, stirring occasionally.
- Add the kale, salt, and pepper and cook for an additional 10 minutes, stirring occasionally, until the lentils and potatoes are tender.
- Serve warm.

Nutrition Facts (per serving): Calories: 184 Total Fat: 2.5g Saturated Fat: 0.3g Cholesterol: 0mg Sodium: 736 mg Carbohydrates: 33.5g Fibre: 8.8g Sugar: 2.6g Protein: 9.7g

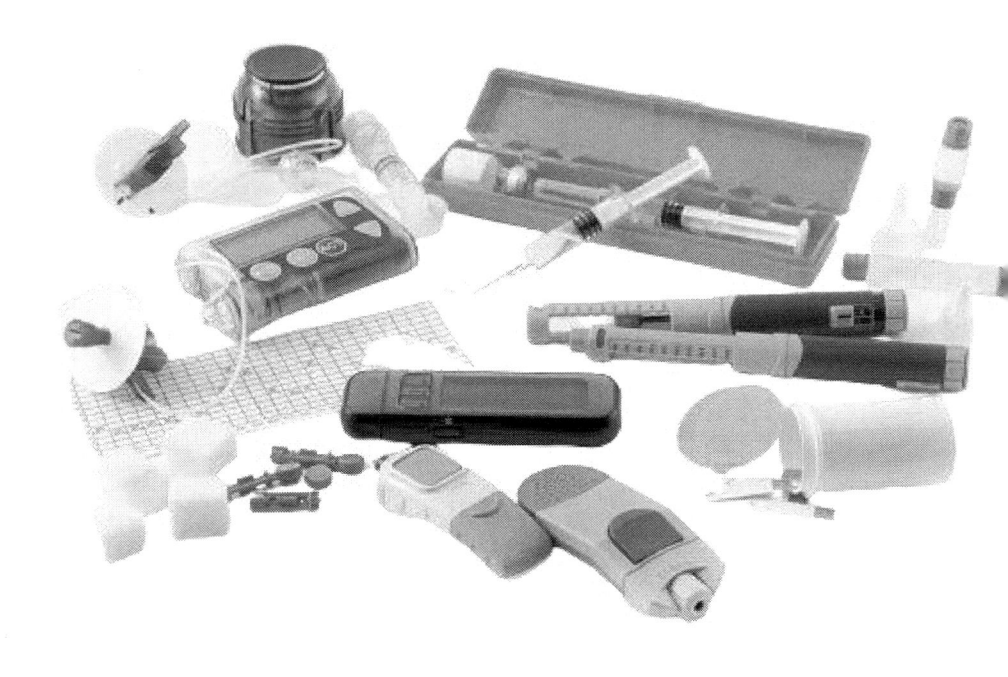

Tuna and White Bean Salad

Preparation Time: 15 minutes

Cooking Time: 20 minutes

Servings: 4

Ingredients:

- 2 cans tuna, drained
- 1 can white beans, drained and rinsed
- 1/2 cup celery, chopped
- 1/4 cup red onion, chopped
- 1/4 cup parsley, chopped
- 2 tablespoons olive oil
- 2 tablespoons lemon juice

- 1 teaspoon dried oregano
- Salt and pepper, to taste

Directions:

> In a large bowl, combine the tuna, beans, celery, onion, and parsley; set aside.

> In a small bowl, whisk together the olive oil, lemon juice, oregano, salt, and pepper.

> Pour the dressing over the tuna and bean mixture and stir to combine.

> Serve chilled or at room temperature.

Nutrients Facts (per serving): Calories: 190 Total Fat: 7g Saturated Fat: 1g Cholesterol: 20mg Sodium: 270mg Total Carbohydrate: 16g Dietary Fibre: 5g Protein: 15g

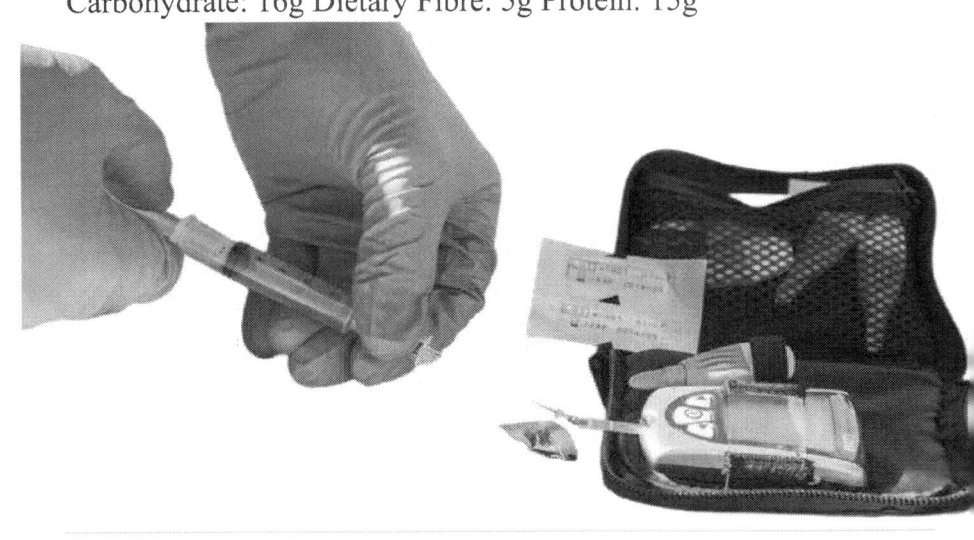

Turkey and Veggie Burger on a Whole Wheat Bun

Preparation Time: 15 minutes

Cooking Time: 10 minutes

Servings: 4

Ingredients:

- 1-pound ground turkey
- ¼ cup diced white onion
- 2 cloves garlic, minced
- ¼ cup grated carrots
- 1 egg

- 1 tablespoon Worcestershire sauce
- 1 teaspoon Italian seasoning
- ¼ teaspoon salt
- 1 tomato, sliced
- ¼ teaspoon pepper
- 4 whole wheat hamburger buns
- 1 teaspoon olive oil

Directions:

- In a medium bowl, combine the ground turkey, onion, garlic, carrots, egg, Worcestershire sauce, Italian seasoning, salt, and pepper.
- Shape the mixture into 4 patties and set aside.
- Heat the olive oil in a large skillet over medium-high heat. Once the oil is hot, add the patties and cook for about 5 minutes on each side, or until the patties are cooked through.
- Toast the buns in the skillet for 1-2 minutes per side.
- Serve the burgers on the toasted buns and enjoy!

Nutritional Facts (per serving): Calories: 320 Fat: 10g Carbohydrates: 29g Protein: 23g Sodium: 410mg Fibre: 4g Sugars: 3g

CHAPTER 4 DINNER RECIPES
Grilled Fish with Sautéed Vegetables

Preparation Time: 15 minutes

Cooking Time: 30 minutes

Servings: 2

Ingredients:

- 2 fillets of fish of your choice
- 1/2 cup of sliced onions
- 1/2 cup of sliced bell peppers
- 1/2 cup of sliced mushrooms
- 2 tablespoons of olive oil
- 2 teaspoons of lemon juice

- Salt and pepper to taste

Directions:

> - Preheat the grill to medium-high heat.
> - Place the fish fillets on the grill and cook for about 5 minutes on each side.
> - In a large skillet, heat the olive oil over medium-high heat.
> - Add the onions, bell peppers, and mushrooms and sauté for about 5 minutes, stirring occasionally.
> - Add the lemon juice and season with salt and pepper to taste.
> - Serve the grilled fish with the sautéed vegetables.

Nutrients Facts (per serving): Calories: 267 Protein: 37 g Carbohydrates: 10 g Fat: 10 g Fibre: 3 g Sodium: 89 mg

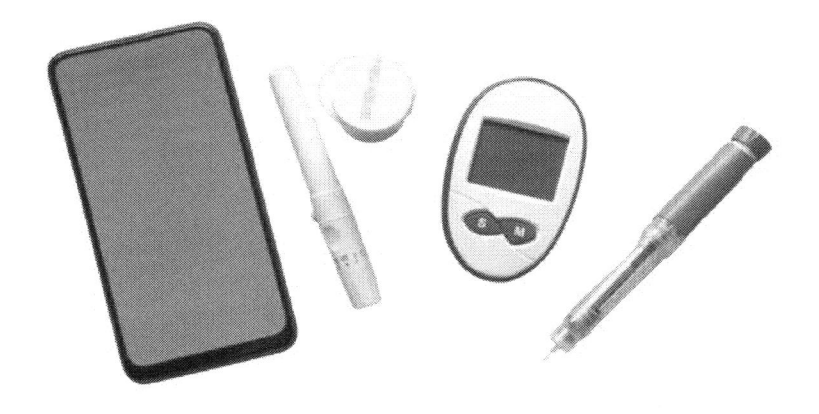

Baked Chicken and Spinach Salad

Preparation Time: 10 minutes

Cooking Time: 30 minutes

Servings: 4

Ingredients:

- 4 boneless and skinless chicken breasts
- 1 tablespoon olive oil
- 1 teaspoon garlic powder
- 1 teaspoon dried oregano
- 2 tablespoons balsamic vinegar
- 4 cups spinach
- 1/2 red onion, thinly sliced

- 1/4 cup feta cheese
- Salt and pepper, to taste

Directions:

➢ Preheat oven to 350 degrees F.

➢ Place chicken breasts in a baking dish. Drizzle with olive oil, garlic powder, and oregano. Bake for 20 minutes or until chicken is cooked through.

➢ Meanwhile, in a large bowl, combine spinach, red onion, feta cheese, and balsamic vinegar. Toss to combine.

➢ Cut cooked chicken into cubes and add to the salad. Season with salt and pepper, to taste.

➢ Serve and enjoy.

Nutrition Facts (per serving): Calories: 220 Carbohydrates: 5 g Protein: 28 g Fat: 8 g Saturated Fat: 2 g Cholesterol: 72 mg Sodium: 179 mg Potassium: 441 mg Fibre: 1 g Sugar: 2 g Calcium: 109 mg Iron: 2 mg

Lentil Soup with Brown Rice

Preparation Time: 5 minutes

Cooking Time: 25 minutes

Servings: 4

Ingredients:

- 2 cups of red lentils
- 2 cups of brown rice
- 2 tablespoons of olive oil
- 1 large onion, diced
- 4 cloves of garlic, minced
- 4 cups of vegetable broth

- 2 teaspoons of ground cumin
- 2 teaspoons of ground coriander
- 1 teaspoon of turmeric
- Salt and pepper to taste

Directions:

- Heat the olive oil in a large pot over medium-high heat.
- Add the diced onion and garlic and sauté until the onion is softened.
- Add the lentils, rice, vegetable broth, cumin, coriander, and turmeric to the pot and stir to combine.
- Bring the soup to a boil, then reduce the heat to low and simmer for 15 minutes, stirring occasionally.
- Season with salt and pepper to taste, then serve hot.

Nutrition Facts (per serving): Calories: 300 Protein: 13 g Total Fat: 5 g Saturated Fat: 1 g Carbohydrates: 44 g Fibre: 10 g Sugar: 2 g Sodium: 310 mg

Roasted Turkey with Sweet Potatoes

Preparation Time: 10 minutes

Cooking Time: 1 hour

Servings: 4

Ingredients:

- 4 lb. turkey, cut into 4 pieces
- 1 large sweet potato, peeled and diced
- 2 tablespoons olive oil
- 1 teaspoon salt
- 1 teaspoon pepper
- 1 teaspoon garlic powder
- 1 teaspoon onion powder
- 1 teaspoon paprika

Directions:

- Preheat the oven to 400 degrees F.
- Place the turkey pieces onto a baking sheet and season with the salt, pepper, garlic powder, onion powder, and paprika.
- In a separate bowl, combine the sweet potatoes and olive oil.
- Place the sweet potatoes around the turkey pieces on the baking sheet.
- Place the baking sheet in the oven and roast for 45 minutes.
- Remove the baking sheet from the oven and turn the turkey pieces and sweet potatoes over.
- Return the baking sheet to the oven and roast for an additional 15 minutes, or until the turkey is cooked through.

Nutrition Facts (per serving): 1/4 of recipe | Calories: 441 | Fat: 17g | Carbohydrates: 24g | Protein: 43g | Sodium: 792mg | Fibre: 3g

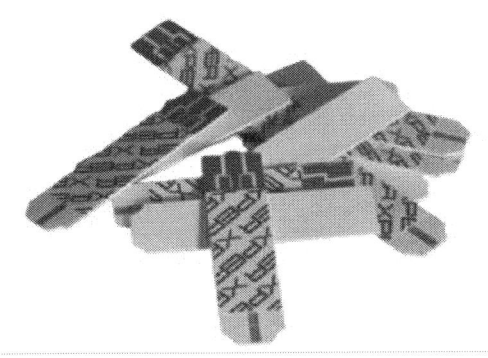

Spaghetti Squash with Marinara Sauce

Preparation Time: 10 minutes

Cooking Time: 45 minutes

Servings: 4

Ingredients:

- 1 spaghetti squash (3-4 pounds)
- 1 tablespoon extra-virgin olive oil
- 1 teaspoon Italian herbs
- 1 ½ cups low-sugar marinara sauce
- 2 tablespoons freshly grated Parmesan cheese

Directions:

- Preheat oven to 375°F.
- Cut squash in half lengthwise and remove the seeds. Place the squash halves cut side down onto a baking sheet.
- Bake for 30-35 minutes or until squash is tender.
- Meanwhile, heat olive oil in a saucepan over medium heat. Add the Italian herbs and stir for 1 minute.
- Add the marinara sauce and bring to a simmer. Simmer for 10 minutes.
- When squash is done, use a fork to scrape the spaghetti-like strands into a bowl.
- Top the squash strands with the marinara sauce and Parmesan cheese.

Nutrients Facts (Per Serving): Calories: 125 kcal Fat: 5 g Carbohydrate: 17 g Fibre: 4 g Protein: 4 g Sugar: 8 g

Grilled Salmon with Roasted Asparagus

Preparation Time: 10 minutes

Cooking Time: 30 minutes

Servings: 4

Ingredients:

- 4 fillets of salmon
- 1 pound of asparagus
- 2 tablespoons of olive oil
- 2 tablespoons of lemon juice
- 2 cloves of garlic, minced
- Salt and pepper to taste

Directions:

- Preheat the oven to 400 degrees Fahrenheit.
- Place salmon fillets on a greased baking sheet.
- Drizzle olive oil and lemon juice over the salmon.
- Sprinkle garlic, salt, and pepper over the salmon.
- Place asparagus on a separate greased baking sheet.
- Drizzle with remaining olive oil and lemon juice.
- Sprinkle it with garlic, salt, and pepper.
- Bake salmon for 15 minutes and asparagus for 10 minutes. Serve and enjoy.

Nutrients Facts (per serving): Calories: 340 kcal Carbohydrates: 6 g Protein: 33 g Fat: 21 g Fibre: 3 g Sodium: 124 mg

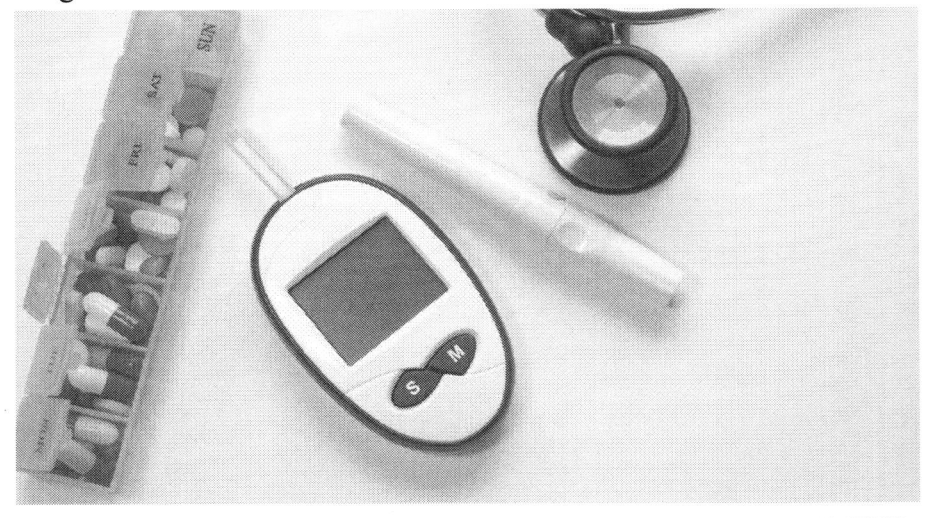

Quinoa Salad with Shrimp

Preparation Time: 15 minutes

Cooking Time: 20 minutes

Servings: 4

Ingredients:

- 1 cup quinoa
- 1/4 cup extra-virgin olive oil
- 1/4 cup fresh lemon juice
- 2 cloves garlic, minced
- 1/4 teaspoon sea salt
- 1/4 teaspoon freshly ground black pepper
- 1/2 cup chopped fresh parsley
- 1/2 cup chopped fresh basil

- 1/2 cup diced red onion
- 1/2 cup diced red bell pepper
- 1/2 cup diced yellow bell pepper
- 1/2 cup diced cucumber
- 12 ounces cooked shrimp, peeled and deveined
- 2 tablespoons capers, drained

Directions:

- In a medium saucepan, bring 2 cups of water to a boil over high heat. Add the quinoa and reduce the heat to low. Simmer, covered, for 15 minutes, or until the quinoa is tender.
- In a large bowl, whisk together the olive oil, lemon juice, garlic, salt, and pepper.
- Add the parsley, basil, onion, bell peppers, cucumber, shrimp, and capers to the bowl and toss to combine.
- Add the cooked quinoa to the bowl and toss to combine.
- Serve warm or chilled.

Nutrition Facts (per serving): Calories: 348 kcal, Carbohydrates: 22.3 g, Protein: 20.9 g, Fat: 18.4 g, Saturated Fat: 2.8 g, Cholesterol: 144 mg, Sodium: 472 mg, Fibre: 3.7 g, Sugar: 3.2 g.

Baked Tilapia with Broccoli

Preparation Time: 10 minutes

Cooking Time: 30 minutes

Servings: 4

Ingredients:

- 4 Tilapia fillets
- 2 tablespoons olive oil
- 2 cloves garlic, minced
- 1/2 teaspoon onion powder
- 1/2 teaspoon dried oregano
- 1/4 teaspoon paprika
- 2 cups fresh broccoli florets

- Salt and pepper, to taste

Directions:

> Preheat oven to 375F.
> Line a baking sheet with parchment paper.
> Place Tilapia fillets on prepared baking sheet and set aside.
> In a small bowl, whisk together olive oil, garlic, onion powder, oregano, and paprika.
> Pour olive oil mixture over Tilapia fillets and spread evenly.
> Place broccoli florets around the Tilapia fillets.
> Sprinkle it with salt and pepper.
> Bake in a preheated oven for 20 minutes, or until fish is cooked through and broccoli is tender.
> Serve and enjoy.

Nutrition Facts (per serving): 1 fillet with broccoli Calories: 191 Total Fat: 8.2g Saturated Fat: 1.2g Cholesterol: 53 mg Sodium: 135mg Total Carbohydrates: 4.3g Dietary Fibre: 2.2g Sugars: 1.3g Protein: 24.2g

Stuffed Peppers with Brown Rice

Preparation Time: 15 minutes

Cooking Time: 45 minutes

Servings: 4

Ingredients:

- 4 large bell peppers
- 2 tablespoons olive oil
- 1 small onion, diced
- 2 cloves garlic, minced
- 1 cup cooked brown rice
- 1 can (15 ounces) black beans, rinsed and drained
- 1 teaspoon cumin
- 1/2 teaspoon chilli powder

- 1/4 teaspoon salt
- 1/4 teaspoon black pepper
- 1 cup shredded cheddar cheese
- 2 tablespoons chopped fresh cilantro
- 1/2 cup salsa

Directions:

- Preheat oven to 375 degrees F.
- Cut off the tops of the peppers, remove the seeds, and discard. Place the peppers in a baking dish.
- Heat the olive oil in a large skillet over medium heat. Add the onion and garlic and cook, stirring, until softened, about 5 minutes.
- Add the cooked rice, beans, cumin, chili powder, salt, and pepper to the skillet and cook, stirring, until heated through, about 5 minutes.
- Remove from heat and stir in the cheese and cilantro.
- Divide the filling among the peppers and top each with 1 tablespoon salsa.
- Bake until the peppers are tender and the filling is hot, about 40 minutes.
- Serve and enjoy.

Nutrition Facts (per serving): Calories: 360 Fat: 15 g Sodium: 500 mg Carbohydrates: 44 g Fibre: 8 g Protein: 12 g

Vegetable Stir Fry

Preparation Time: 10 minutes

Cooking Time: 10 minutes

Servings: 4

Ingredients:

- 2 tablespoons olive oil
- 1 onion, diced

- 2 cloves garlic, minced
- 2 cups broccoli florets
- 1 red bell pepper, diced
- 1/2 cup carrots, julienned
- 1/2 cup snow peas
- 2 tablespoons low-sodium soy sauce
- 1/4 teaspoon sesame oil
- 2 tablespoons fresh, chopped parsley

Directions:

- Heat the olive oil in a large skillet over medium heat.
- Add the diced onion and garlic and sauté for a few minutes until softened.
- Add the broccoli, bell pepper, carrots, and snow peas and stir-fry for 5 minutes.
- Add the low-sodium soy sauce and sesame oil, stirring to combine.
- Cook for another few minutes until the vegetables are tender-crisp.
- Remove from heat and sprinkle with chopped parsley before serving.

Nutritional Facts (per serving): 1/4 of recipe Calories: 122 Total Fat: 7g Saturated Fat: 1g Cholesterol: 0mg Sodium: 270mg Carbohydrates: 11g Fibre: 3g Sugar: 4g Protein: 4g

Baked Sweet Potato Fries

Preparation Time: 10 minutes

Cooking Time: 25 minutes

Servings: 4

Ingredients:

- 2 large sweet potatoes, peeled and cut into thin strips
- 2 tablespoons olive oil

- 1 teaspoon garlic powder
- 1 teaspoon paprika
- Salt and pepper, to taste

Directions:

> Preheat oven to 450°F. Line a baking sheet with foil and lightly spray with cooking spray.
> Place sweet potato strips on the baking sheet and drizzle with olive oil. Sprinkle with garlic powder, paprika, salt, and pepper.
> Toss with your hands to evenly coat the sweet potatoes.
> Bake for 20-25 minutes, until sweet potatoes are golden brown and crispy.
> Serve and Enjoy

Nutrition Facts (per serving): Calories: 130 Total Fat: 5g Saturated Fat: 1g Cholesterol: 0mg Sodium: 90mg Total Carbohydrate: 19g Dietary Fibre: 3g Sugars: 4g Protein: 2g

Grilled Chicken with Quinoa

Preparation Time: 10 minutes

Cooking Time: 10 minutes

Servings: 4

Ingredients:

- 4 boneless, skinless chicken breasts
- 2 tablespoons olive oil
- 1 teaspoon garlic powder
- 1 teaspoon paprika
- 1 teaspoon black pepper
- 1 teaspoon dried oregano
- 1 teaspoon sea salt

- 1 cup quinoa
- 2 cups chicken broth

Directions:

- Preheat the grill to medium-high heat.
- In a small bowl, mix together olive oil, garlic powder, paprika, pepper, oregano, and salt.
- Rub the chicken breasts with the olive oil mixture and place on the preheated grill. Grill for about 5 minutes per side, or until the chicken is cooked through.
- Meanwhile, in a medium saucepan, bring the chicken broth to a boil. Add the quinoa and reduce the heat to low.
- Simmer for 10 minutes, or until all the liquid is absorbed.
- Serve the grilled chicken with the quinoa.

Nutrition Facts (per serving): 1 serving Calories: 353 Total Fat: 8.2 g Saturated Fat: 1.3 g Cholesterol: 66 mg Sodium: 654 mg Total Carbohydrates: 37 g Dietary Fibre: 4.6 g Protein: 28 g

Chickpea and Butternut Squash Curry

Preparation Time: 10 minutes

Cooking Time: 30 minutes

Servings: 4

Ingredients:

- 1 tbsp. olive oil
- 1 onion, diced
- 2 cloves garlic, minced
- 1 tsp ground coriander
- 1 tsp ground cumin
- 2 tsp gram masala
- 1/2 tsp ground turmeric

- 1/4 tsp chili powder
- 1/4 tsp cayenne pepper
- 1 can chickpeas, drained and rinsed
- 2 cups butternut squash, cubed
- 1 can diced tomatoes
- 2 cups vegetable broth
- 1/2 cup coconut milk
- 2 tbsp. chopped fresh cilantro, for garnish

Directions:

> Heat the olive oil in a large pot over medium heat. Add the onion and garlic and sauté until softened and fragrant, about 5 minutes.

> Add the coriander, cumin, gram masala, turmeric, chili powder, and cayenne pepper and cook, stirring frequently, for another minute.

> Add the chickpeas, butternut squash, diced tomatoes, vegetable broth, and coconut milk and bring to a boil. Lower the heat and simmer for 15 minutes, or until the butternut squash is tender.

> Serve the curry with fresh cilantro and naan or rice, if desired. Enjoy!

Nutrients Facts (per serving): Calories: 219 Fat: 11 g Carbohydrates: 28 g Protein: 6 g Fibre: 5 g Sugar: 6 g Sodium: 164 mg

Greek Salad with Tuna

Preparation Time: 15 minutes

Cooking Time: 15 minutes

Servings: 4

Ingredients:

- 4 cups chopped Romaine lettuce
- 1 cup cherry tomatoes, halved
- 1/2 red onion, thinly sliced

- 1/2 cucumber, chopped
- 1/3 cup Kalamata olives
- 1/3 cup crumbled feta cheese
- 1 (5-ounce) can tuna, drained
- 2 tablespoons extra virgin olive oil
- tablespoon red wine vinegar
- 1 teaspoon dried oregano
- Salt and pepper to taste

Directions:

- In a large bowl, combine lettuce, tomatoes, red onion, cucumber, olives, feta cheese, and tuna.
- In a small bowl, whisk together olive oil, red wine vinegar, oregano, salt, and pepper.
- Drizzle the dressing over the salad and toss to combine.

Nutrients Facts (per serving): Calories: 169 Total Fat: 10g Saturated Fat: 3g Cholesterol: 16 mg Sodium: 286 mg Carbohydrates: 8g Fibre: 2g Protein: 11g

Turkey Burger with Lettuce and Tomato

Preparation Time: 10 minutes

Cooking Time: 15 minutes

Servings: 1

Ingredients:

- 2 tablespoons olive oil
- 1/4-pound ground turkey
- Salt and pepper to taste
- 1 whole wheat hamburger bun
- 1 slice of tomato
- 2 lettuce leaves
- 1 tablespoon low-fat mayonnaise

Directions:

- Heat 1 tablespoon of olive oil in a large skillet over medium heat.
- Add the ground turkey, and season with salt and pepper. Cook for about 8 minutes, stirring often, until the turkey is cooked through.
- Toast the hamburger bun.
- Spread mayonnaise on the toasted bun.
- Place the cooked turkey on the bun, and top with lettuce and tomato.
- Drizzle the remaining 1 tablespoon of olive oil over the lettuce and tomato.
- Serve immediately.

Nutrition Facts (per serving): Calories: 454 Fat: 24.3 g

Carbohydrates: 34.2 g Protein: 27.2 g Fibre: 4.2 g Sugar: 4.9 g Sodium: 586 mg

CHAPTER 5 SNACKS RECIPES

High-fibre crackers with peanut butter

Preparation Time: 10 minutes

Cooking Time: 20 minutes

Servings: 1

Ingredients:

- 2 high-fibre crackers
- 1 tablespoon of natural peanut butter

Directions:

➢ Take 2 high-fibre crackers and spread 1 tablespoon of natural peanut butter on each cracker.

➢ Enjoy your snack!

Nutrient Facts (per serving): Calories: 220 Protein: 8 grams Carbohydrates: 25 grams Fibre: 8 grams Fat: 12 grams Sugar: 4 grams

Air-popped popcorn

Preparation Time: 5 minutes

Cooking Time: 5 minutes

Servings: 1

Ingredients:

- 1/4 cup popcorn kernels
- 1 tablespoon vegetable oil
- Salt, to taste

Directions:

- Heat 1 tablespoon of vegetable oil in a large pot over medium-high heat.
- Once the oil is hot, add in 1/4 cup of popcorn kernels and stir to combine.
- Cover the pot with a lid and allow the popcorn to cook, shaking the pot occasionally, until all of the kernels have popped, approximately 3-5 minutes.
- Once the popcorn is done popping, remove from heat and season with salt to taste.

Nutrition Facts (per serving): Calories: 109 Fat: 5.2 g Carbohydrates: 14.7 g Protein: 2.7 g Fibre: 3.6 g Sugar: 0 g Sodium: 2 mg

Greek yoghourt with berries

Preparation Time: 5 minutes

Cooking Time: 10 minutes

Servings: 1

Ingredients:

- 1/2 cup plain Greek yogurt
- 1/4 cup of fresh or frozen berries of your choice

Directions:

- In a bowl, combine the Greek yogurt and berries.
- Mix together until the berries are evenly distributed in the yogurt.

➢ Serve immediately and enjoy!

Nutritional Facts (per serving): Calories: 130 kcal Carbohydrates: 12 g Protein: 14 g Fat: 2 g Sodium: 65 mg Sugar: 10 g

Celery sticks with hummus

Preparation Time: 10 minutes

Cooking Time: 0 minutes

Servings: 2

Ingredients:

- 2 stalks of celery
- 2 tablespoons of hummus
- Salt and pepper to taste

Directions:

- Wash and cut the celery into sticks.
- Place the celery sticks on a plate.
- Spoon the hummus onto the celery sticks.
- Sprinkle salt and pepper to taste.
- Serve and enjoy.

Nutrition Facts (per serving): Calories: 85 kcal Total Fat: 3.8g Total Carbohydrates: 9.2g Protein: 2.6g Sodium: 288mg Fibre: 2.6g Sugar: 2.3g

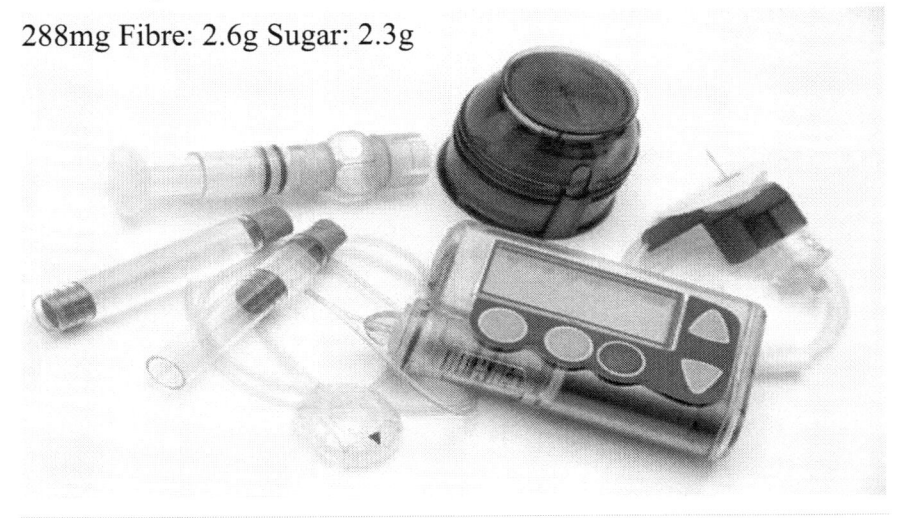

Apple slices with almond butter

Preparation Time: 10 minutes

Cooking Time: 2 minutes

Servings: 1

Ingredients:

- 1 Apple, sliced
- 2 tablespoons almond butter

Directions:

- ➢ Slice the apple into thin slices.
- ➢ Spread the almond butter onto the slices.
- ➢ Place the slices onto a plate and microwave for 2 minutes.

> Enjoy!

Nutrition Facts (per serving): Calories: 246 Fat: 13.3g Carbohydrates: 31.1g Protein: 4.7g Fibre: 6.3g

Edamame

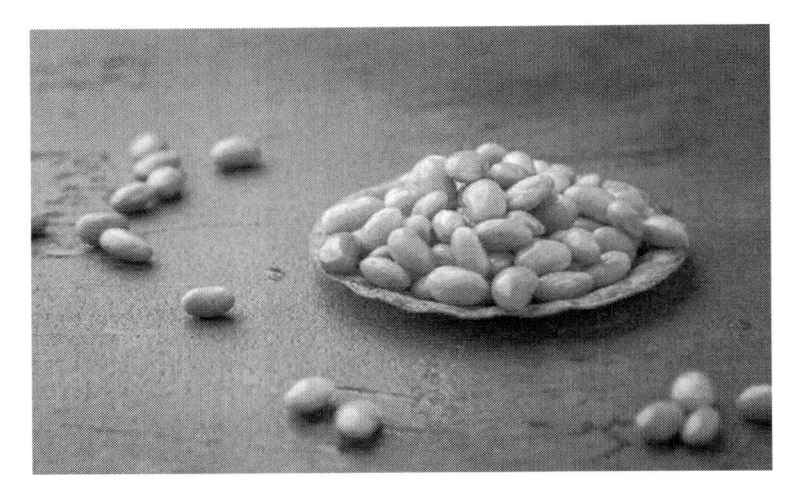

Preparation Time: 10 minutes

Cooking Time: 5 minutes

Servings: 4

Ingredients:

- 2 cups frozen edamame
- 2 tablespoons olive oil
- Salt to taste

Directions:

- Preheat oven to 375 degrees F.
- Place edamame in a bowl and add olive oil, salt and any other desired seasonings. Stir to combine.
- Spread edamame onto a baking sheet and bake for 5 minutes.
- Remove from oven and serve.

Nutrition Facts (per serving): Calories: 90 Fat: 5g Carbohydrates: 4g Protein: 7g Fibre: 2g

Nuts and seeds

Preparation Time: 10 minutes

Cooking Time: 15 minutes

Servings: 2

Ingredients:

- 2 tablespoons of chia seeds
- 2 tablespoons of pumpkin seeds
- 2 tablespoons of sunflower seeds
- 2 tablespoons of walnuts
- 2 tablespoons of almonds
- 2 tablespoons of cashew nuts

- 2 tablespoons of sesame seeds

Directions:

> Preheat a large skillet over medium-high heat.
> Add all the nuts and seeds to the skillet and toast until golden brown, stirring occasionally.
> Remove from heat and transfer to a bowl.
> Enjoy!

Nutrients Facts (per serving): Calories: 320 kcal Fat: 23.6 g Carbohydrates: 16.8 g Protein: 11.2 g Fibre: 7.2 g Sugar: 0.3 g

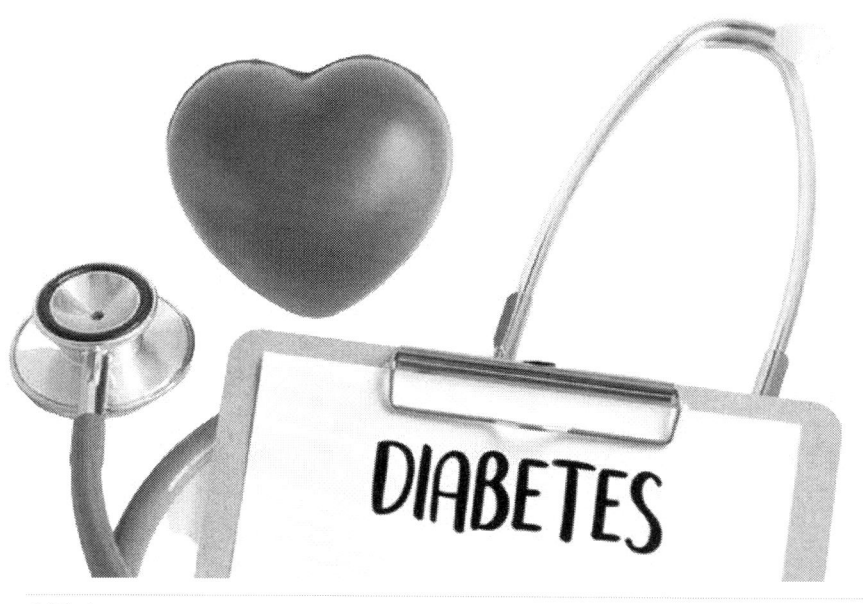

Trail mix with dried fruit

Preparation Time: 5 minutes

Cooking Time: 10 minutes

Servings: 2

Ingredients:

- ½ cup of almonds
- ½ cup of walnuts
- ½ cup of unsalted peanuts
- ½ cup of dried cranberries
- ½ cup of raisins
- ½ cup of pumpkin seeds
- ¼ teaspoon of sea salt

Directions:

- Preheat oven to 350°F.
- Spread the almonds, walnuts, peanuts, cranberries, raisins, and pumpkin seeds on a baking sheet.
- Roast in the oven for 5 minutes.
- Remove from oven and transfer to a bowl.
- Add the sea salt and mix well.
- Serve and enjoy!

Nutrition Facts (per serving): Calories: 370 Fat:
17g Carbohydrates: 37g Protein: 14g Sodium: 200mg

Sugar: 20g

Cottage cheese with fruit

Preparation Time: 5 minutes

Cooking Time: 10 minutes

Servings: 2

Ingredients:

- 1/2 cup low-fat cottage cheese
- 1/2 cup fresh diced strawberries
- 1/2 cup fresh diced pineapple
- 1/4 cup diced kiwi
- 1/4 cup diced mangos
- 2 tablespoons honey

Directions:

- In a medium bowl, combine the cottage cheese and diced fruit.
- Drizzle the honey over the top of the mixture and stir to combine.
- Divide the mixture evenly between two bowls and serve.

Nutrition Facts (per serving): Calories: 250 Total Fat: 2.5g Saturated Fat: 1.5g Cholesterol: 10mg Sodium: 200mg

Total Carbohydrates: 40g Dietary Fibre: 4g Sugars: 30g

Protein: 16g

Whole-grain toast with avocado

Preparation Time: 10 minutes

Complete Time: 15 minutes

Servings: 1

Ingredients:

- 1 slice whole-grain bread
- ½ avocado
- 1 teaspoon olive oil
- Salt and pepper to taste

Directions:

> Toast the slice of whole-grain bread.

- Remove the avocado from its skin and pit, and mash it with a fork.
- Spread the mashed avocado onto the toasted bread.
- Drizzle the olive oil over the top of the avocado.
- Sprinkle salt and pepper to taste.

Nutrient Facts (per serving): Calories: 227 Total Fat: 14g Saturated Fat: 2g Cholesterol: 0mg Sodium: 141mg

Total Carbohydrates: 23g Dietary Fibre: 7g Sugar: 1g

Protein: 7g

Cucumber slices with tuna

Preparation Time: 5 minutes

Cooking Time: 10 minutes

Servings: 1

Ingredients:

- 1 cucumber
- 1 can light tuna
- 2 tablespoons of mayonnaise
- 1 teaspoon of lemon juice
- Salt and pepper to taste

Directions:

- Cut the cucumber into thin slices.
- In a bowl, mix the tuna, mayonnaise, lemon juice, salt, and pepper.
- Spread the tuna mixture on top of the cucumber slices.
- Serve chilled.

Nutrition Facts (per serving): Calories: 200 Fat: 10 g Carbohydrates: 10 g Protein: 20 g Sodium: 400 mg

Roasted chickpeas

Preparation Time: 10 minutes

Cooking Time: 25 minutes

Servings: 4

Ingredients:

- 2 cups chickpeas
- 1 tablespoon olive oil
- 1 teaspoon garlic powder
- 1 teaspoon paprika
- ½ teaspoon salt

Directions:

- Preheat the oven to 400 degrees Fahrenheit.
- Rinse and drain chickpeas, then spread them out on a baking sheet.
- Drizzle the olive oil over the chickpeas, then sprinkle garlic powder, paprika, and salt on top.
- Use your hands to mix the seasonings into the chickpeas until they are all coated.
- Roast the chickpeas in the oven for 20-25 minutes, stirring once halfway through.
- Serve warm and enjoy!

Nutrients Facts (per serving): Calories: 128 kcal Fat: 4.3 g Carbohydrates: 18.6 g Protein: 5.2 g Fibre: 5.8 g

Hard-boiled eggs

Preparation Time: 5 minutes

Cooking Time: 15 minutes

Servings: 4

Ingredients:

- 4 large eggs

Directions:

- ➢ Place eggs in a single layer in a pot and add enough cold water to cover the eggs by 1 inch.
- ➢ Place the pot over high heat and bring to a rolling boil.
- ➢ Remove pot from heat, cover, and let sit for 12 minutes.

- Drain the hot water from the pot and run cold water over the eggs until they are completely cooled.
- Peel eggs and serves, or store for later use.

Nutrition Facts (per serving): Calories: 78 Total Fat: 5g Saturated Fat: 1.5g Cholesterol: 186 mg Sodium: 62 mg Total Carbohydrates: 0.6g Protein: 6.3g

Low-fat string cheese

Preparation Time: 5 minutes

Cooking Time: 15 minutes

Servings: 1

Ingredients:

- 2 tablespoons of low-fat cream cheese
- 2 tablespoons of low-fat milk
- 2 tablespoons of grated low-fat cheddar cheese
- 1/4 teaspoon of garlic powder
- 1/4 teaspoon of onion powder
- Salt to taste

Directions:

- In a bowl, combine the cream cheese, milk, cheddar cheese, garlic powder, onion powder, and salt.
- Mix until everything is well combined.
- Take a tablespoon of the mixture and roll it into a ball.
- Place the ball of cheese on a parchment-lined baking sheet.
- Repeat the process until all of the cheese mixture has been used up.
- Place the baking sheet in the fridge and chill for at least 15 minutes.
- Once chilled, your low-fat string cheese is ready to enjoy!

Nutritional Facts (per serving): Calories: 75 Fat: 2.5g Carbohydrates: 1.5g Protein: 8.5g Sodium: 115mg

Protein smoothie with almond milk

Preparation Time: 10 minutes

Cooking Time: 10 minutes

Servings: 1

Ingredients:

- 1 cup of unsweetened almond milk
- 1 scoop of protein powder
- 1 tablespoon of natural peanut butter
- 1/2 frozen banana
- 1/4 cup of frozen strawberries

Directions:

- In a blender, combine the almond milk, protein powder, peanut butter, banana, and strawberries.
- Blend until the mixture is smooth and creamy.
- Pour into a glass and enjoy.

Nutrition Facts (per serving): Calories: 241 Total Fat: 8 g Saturated Fat: 1 g Cholesterol: 0 mg Sodium: 293 mg Total Carbohydrates: 19 g Dietary Fibre: 5 g Sugars: 8 g Protein: 21 g

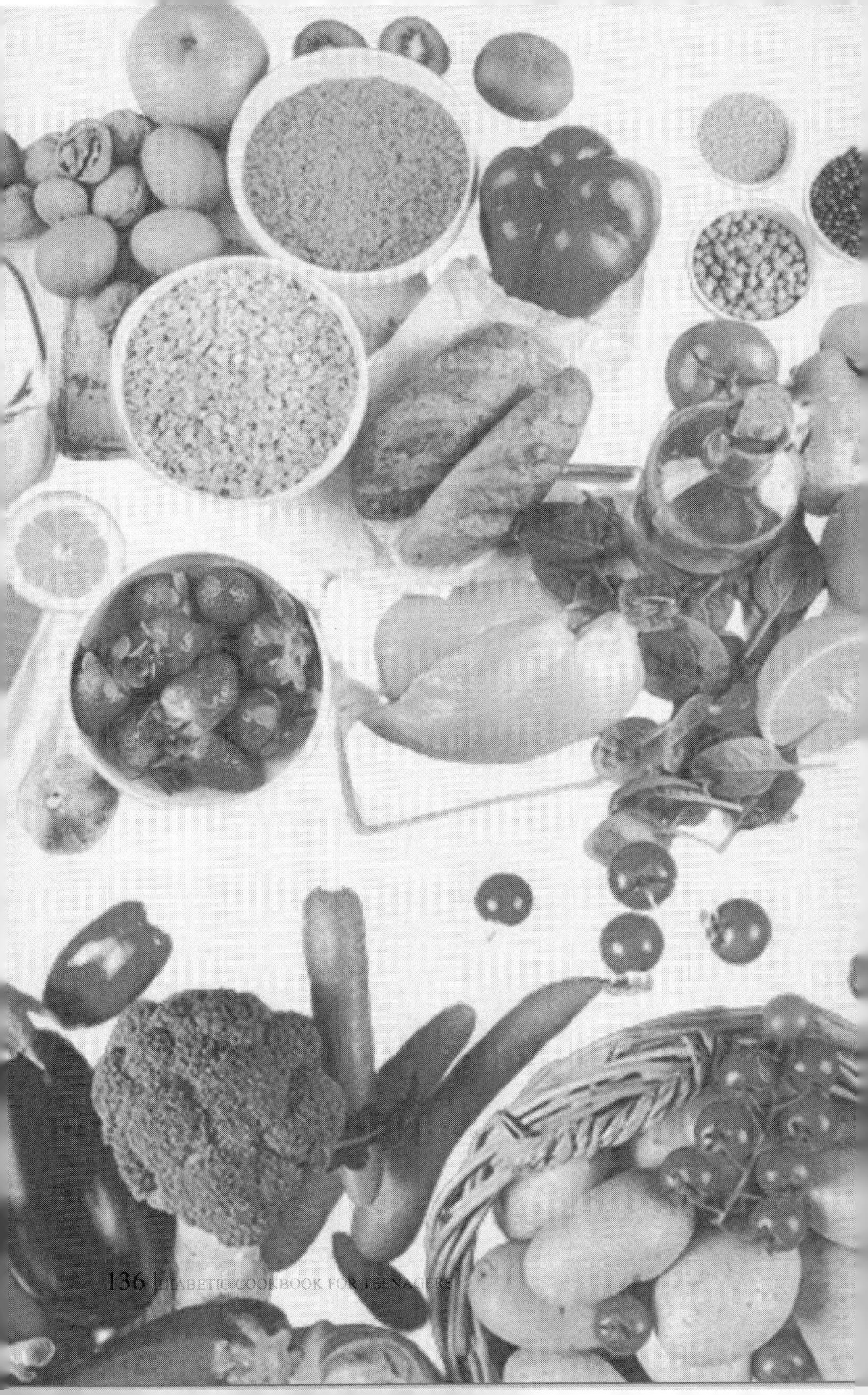

CHAPTER 6 DESSERT RECIPES

Apple slices with cinnamon

Preparation Time: 10 minutes

Cooking Time: 10 minutes

Servings: 4

Ingredients:

- 4 apples
- 2 tablespoons sugar
- 2 tablespoons cinnamon

- 2 tablespoons butter
- 1/4 cup water

Directions:

> Preheat oven to 375°F.
> Place the apple slices in a baking dish.
> In a small bowl, mix together the butter, cinnamon, sugar and raisins (if desired).
> Spread the mixture over the apple slices.
> Bake for 10 minutes, or until the apples are tender.
> Serve warm and enjoy.

Nutrition Facts (per serving): Serving Size: 1/4 of recipe Calories: 125 Total Fat: 5 g Saturated Fat: 3 g Cholesterol: 15 mg Sodium: 0 mg Total Carbohydrates: 21 g Fibre: 2 g Sugar: 17 g Protein: 0 g

Frozen yogurt

Preparation Time: 5 minutes

Cooking Time: 10 minutes

Servings: 4

Ingredients:

- 2 cups of low-fat Greek yogurt
- 2 tablespoons of honey
- 1 teaspoon of vanilla extract
- 1/4 cup of fresh blueberries
- 1/4 cup of chopped strawberries

Directions:

- In a medium bowl, combine the Greek yogurt, honey, and vanilla extract.
- Mix until all the ingredients are combined.
- Add the blueberries and strawberries and mix until all the fruit is evenly distributed.
- Place the mixture in a shallow dish and freeze for at least 10 minutes.
- When frozen, scoop out and serve.

Nutrition Facts (per serving): Calories: 97 Fat: 0g Carbohydrates: 14g Protein: 8g Fibre: 1g Sodium: 35mg

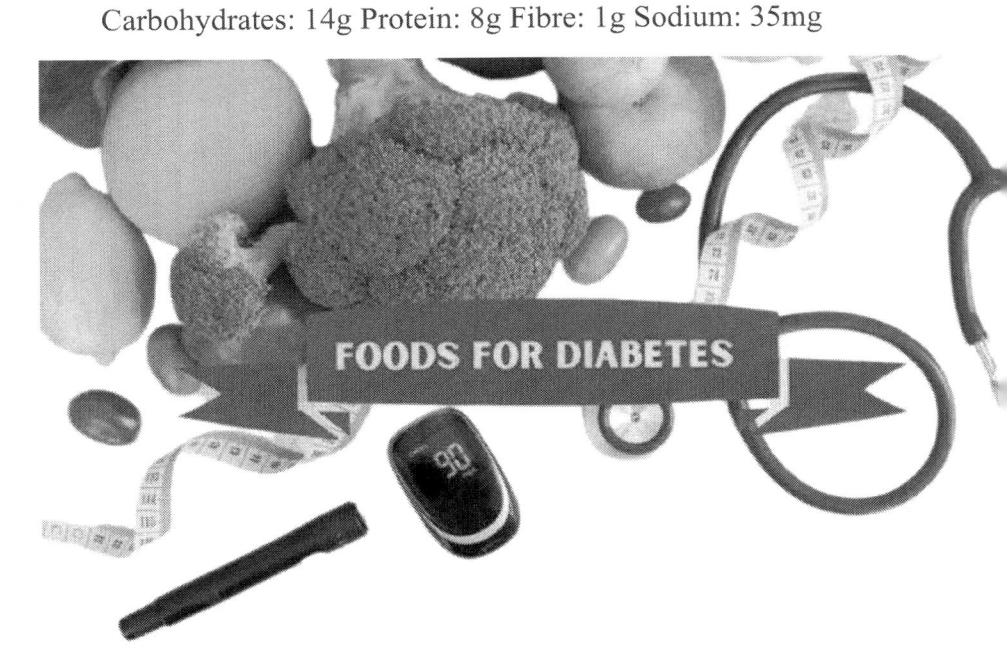

Baked pears with cinnamon

Preparation Time: 5 minutes

Cooking Time: 25 minutes

Servings: 4 servings

Ingredients:

- 4 ripe pears
- 2 tablespoons light brown sugar
- 2 tablespoons honey
- 1 teaspoon cinnamon
- 2 tablespoons butter, melted

Directions:

- ➤ Preheat the oven to 375°F.
- ➤ Cut the pears in half and remove the core.
- ➤ In a small bowl, mix together the light brown sugar, honey, cinnamon, and butter.
- ➤ Place the pears in a baking dish and pour the mixture over the pears.
- ➤ Bake for 25 minutes, or until the pears are tender and the sauce is bubbling.
- ➤ Serve warm.

Nutrition Facts (per serving): 1/4 of recipe Calories: 145 kcal Fat: 5g Carbohydrates: 28g Protein: 1g Sodium: 10mg Sugar: 21g Fibre: 4g

Sugar-free pudding

Preparation Time: 5 minutes

Cooking Time: 10 minutes

Servings: 4 Servings

Ingredients:

- 2 tablespoons of corn-starch
- 2 cups of unsweetened almond milk
- 2 teaspoons of vanilla extract
- 1 teaspoon of ground cinnamon
- 2 tablespoons of Stevia or other sugar substitute
- 2 tablespoons of butter

Directions:

- In a medium saucepan over medium heat, whisk together the corn-starch and almond milk until combined.
- Add in the vanilla extract, ground cinnamon, and Stevia or other sugar substitute and whisk until all ingredients are combined.
- Increase the heat to medium-high and bring the mixture to a low boil.
- Reduce the heat to low and simmer for 5 minutes, stirring occasionally.
- Remove the pudding from the heat and stir in the butter until melted.
- Pour the pudding into individual serving dishes and let cool for 10 minutes before serving.

Nutrition Facts (per serving): 1/4 of the recipe Calories: 89 Fat: 7 g Sodium: 64 mg Carbohydrates: 4.6 g Fibre: 0.6 g Protein: 1.8 g

Baked apples with raisins and cinnamon

Preparation Time: 10 minutes

Cooking Time: 45 minutes

Servings: 2

Ingredients:

- 2 Apples, cored and sliced into wedges
- 2 tablespoons Raisins
- 2 tablespoons Brown sugar
- 1 teaspoon Ground cinnamon
- 1/4 teaspoon Nutmeg
- 2 tablespoons Unsalted Butter, melted

Directions:

- Preheat oven to 375°F.
- Place the apple wedges in an 8x8 inch baking dish.
- In a small bowl, mix together the raisins, brown sugar, cinnamon, and nutmeg.
- Sprinkle the mixture over the apples and drizzle with melted butter.
- Bake for 45 minutes, or until apples are tender.

Nutrients Facts (per serving): Calories: 126 kcal, Carbohydrates: 19 g, Protein: 1 g, Fat: 6 g, Saturated Fat: 4 g, Cholesterol: 15 mg, Sodium: 3 mg, Potassium: 91 mg, fibre: 2 g, Sugar: 15 g, Vitamin A: 215 IU, Vitamin C: 4 mg, Calcium: 20 mg, Iron: 0.6 mg.

Angel food cake

Preparation Time: 20 minutes

Cooking Time: 45 minutes

Servings: 10

Ingredients:

- 1 cup granulated sugar
- 1 cup cake flour
- 1 teaspoon cream of tartar
- 4. ½ teaspoon salt
- 1 cup egg whites
- 1 teaspoon vanilla extract
- ¼ teaspoon almond extract

Direction:

- Preheat oven to 350°F. Grease and flour a 9-inch tube pan.
- In a medium bowl, sift together the sugar, cake flour, cream of tartar, and salt.
- In a separate bowl, combine the egg whites and extracts. Beat the egg whites until they form soft peaks.
- Slowly add the dry ingredients to the egg whites, folding gently until just combined.
- Pour the batter into the prepared tube pan, and bake for 45 minutes, or until the top of the cake is golden brown and a toothpick inserted into the centre comes out clean.
- Let cool in the pan for 10 minutes, then invert onto a wire rack to cool completely.

Nutrients Facts (per serving): Calories: 123 Fat: 0 g Carbohydrates: 26 g Protein: 4 g fibre: 0 g Sugar: 18 g Sodium: 115 mg

Sugar-free cookies

Preparation Time: 10 minutes

Cooking Time: 20 minutes

Servings: 15

Ingredients:

- 1 cup of all-purpose flour
- ½ cup of unsalted butter
- ¼ cup of sugar-free sweetener
- 1 egg
- ½ teaspoon of baking powder
- 1 teaspoon of vanilla extract
- ¼ teaspoon of salt

Directions:

- Preheat oven to 350°F (175°C).
- In a bowl, cream together the butter and sugar-free sweetener until light and fluffy.
- Beat in the egg and mix until combined.
- In a separate bowl, mix together the flour, baking powder, and salt.
- Slowly add the dry ingredients to the wet ingredients and mix until combined.
- Add the vanilla extract and mix until combined.
- Grease a baking sheet with butter or non-stick spray.
- Using a spoon or a cookie scoop, drop spoonful of the cookie dough onto the prepared baking sheet.
- Bake for 8-10 minutes, or until the edges are lightly golden brown.
- Let the cookies cool for a few minutes before transferring them to a wire rack to cool completely.

Nutrition Facts (per serving): 1 cookie Calories: 63 Fat: 4g Carbohydrates: 5g fibre: 0.5g Protein: 1g

Sugar-free ice cream

Preparation Time: 10 minutes

Cooking Time: 35 minutes

Servings: 8

Ingredients:

- 1/2 cup non-fat dry milk powder
- 1/2 cup low-fat cream cheese
- 1/2 cup fat-free sweetened condensed milk
- 1/2 teaspoon vanilla extract
- 1/4 teaspoon almond extract
- 1/4 teaspoon salt

- 1/4 teaspoon liquid stevia
- 2 cups heavy cream
- 1/4 cup chopped almonds, for garnish

Directions:

> In a medium bowl, whisk together the dry milk powder, cream cheese, condensed milk, vanilla, almond extract, salt, and stevia until smooth.

> In a medium saucepan, heat the cream over medium-high heat until steaming. Gradually whisk in the milk mixture. Cook, stirring constantly, until the mixture thickens and coats the back of a spoon, about 5 minutes.

> Pour the mixture into a 9-inch square baking dish and cover with plastic wrap. Refrigerate for at least 4 hours.

> Once the mixture is chilled, transfer it to an ice cream maker and churn according to the manufacturer's instructions. Stir in the almonds.

> Serve immediately or transfer to an airtight container and freeze for up to 1 month.

Nutrition Facts (per serving): Calories: 150 Fat: 8g Carbohydrates: 10g Fibre: 0g Sugar: 8g Protein: 5g

Sugar-free gelatine

Preparation Time: 10 minutes

Cooking Time: 3 hours

Servings: 8

Ingredients:

- 2 packets of sugar-free gelatine
- 2 1/2 cups cold water
- 2 cups boiling water

Directions:

➢ Start by pouring the cold water into a medium-sized bowl.
➢ Add the two packets of sugar-free gelatine to the cold water and stir until the gelatine has completely dissolved.

- Pour the boiling water into the mixture and stir until it is completely combined.
- Pour the mixture into a 9x13 inch dish and place in the refrigerator for at least three hours.
- Cut into 8 slices and serve.

Nutrition Facts (per serving): Calories: 35 Fat: 0g Carbohydrates: 8g Sugar: 0g Protein: 2g

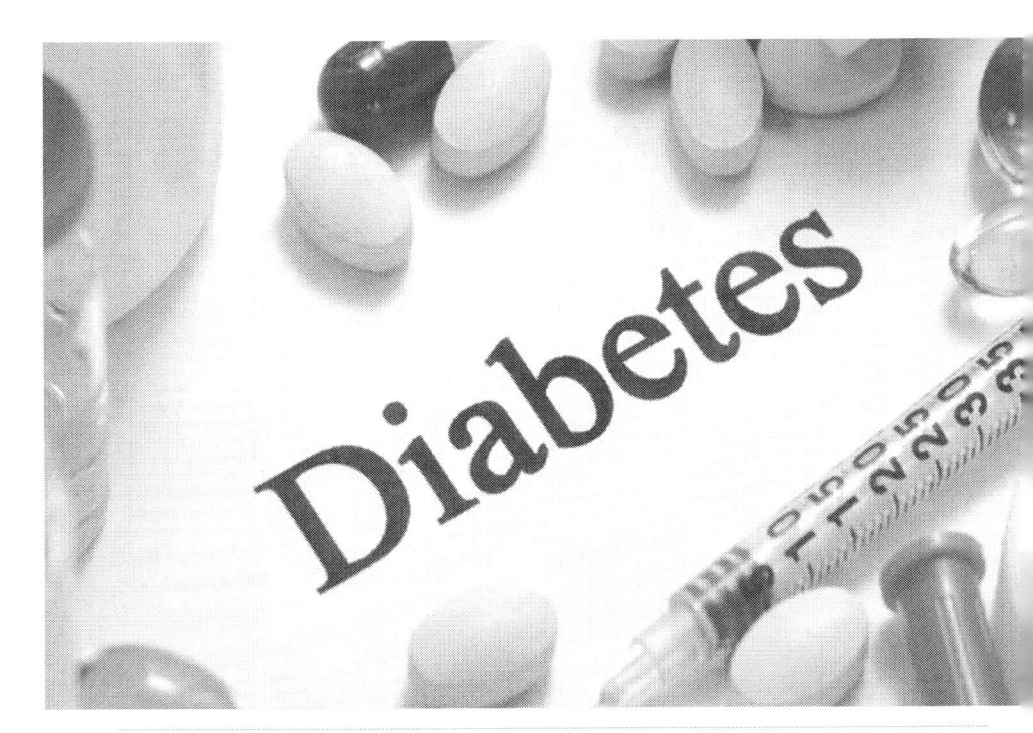

Baked oatmeal with dried fruit

Preparation Time: 10 minutes

Cooking Time: 45 minutes

Servings: 6

Ingredients:

- 2 cups rolled oats
- 2 teaspoons baking powder
- 1 teaspoon ground cinnamon
- 1/4 teaspoon salt
- 1/4 cup honey
- 1/4 cup brown sugar
- 2 tablespoons vegetable oil
- 2 eggs

- 1 cup almond milk
- 1/2 cup dried fruit (raisins, cranberries, cherries, blueberries, etc.)

Directions:

- ➢ Preheat oven to 375 degrees F. Grease an 8-inch square baking dish.
- ➢ In a medium bowl, combine rolled oats, baking powder, cinnamon, and salt.
- ➢ In a separate bowl, whisk together honey, brown sugar, vegetable oil, eggs, and almond milk.
- ➢ Pour wet ingredients into the dry ingredients and stir until well combined.
- ➢ Fold in dried fruit.
- ➢ Pour mixture into prepared baking dish and spread evenly.
- ➢ Bake for 30 minutes or until top is golden brown and oatmeal is set.
- ➢ Enjoy warm with a dollop of yogurt or cream.

Nutrients Facts (per serving): Calories: 221

Carbohydrates: 33g Fat: 7g Protein: 5g Fibre: 3g Sugar: 19g

Sugar-free brownies

Preparation Time: 10 minutes

Cooking Time: 25 minutes

Servings: 16

Ingredients:

- 2/3 cup butter
- 2/3 cup unsweetened cocoa powder
- 1 cup sugar-free granulated sweetener
- 2 large eggs
- 1 teaspoon vanilla extract
- 1/2 cup all-purpose flour
- 1/4 teaspoon salt

Directions:

- Preheat oven to 350 degrees F (175 degrees C). Grease an 8 inch or 9-inch square pan.
- In a large saucepan, melt butter over low heat. Remove from heat, and stir in cocoa and sweetener. Beat in eggs one at a time, then stir in vanilla. Combine flour and salt; stir into the cocoa mixture. Spread batter into prepared pan.
- Bake in preheated oven for 25 to 30 minutes. Do not overcook. Cool in pan on a wire rack. Cut into 16 squares.

Nutrition Facts (per serving): Calories: 84 Total Fat: 5g Saturated Fat: 3g Cholesterol: 25mg Sodium: 75mg Total Carbohydrates: 8g Fibre: 1g Sugars: 0g Protein: 2g

Baked sweet potatoes with cinnamon

Preparation Time: 10 minutes

Cooking Time: 55 minutes

Servings: 4

Ingredients:

- 4 medium sweet potatoes
- 2 tablespoons melted butter
- 2 tablespoons honey
- 1 teaspoon ground cinnamon

Directions:

- Preheat oven to 400 degrees Fahrenheit.
- Scrub sweet potatoes and pat dry.
- Place sweet potatoes on baking sheet lined with parchment paper.
- Bake for 50 minutes or until tender when pierced with a fork.
- Remove from oven and let cool for 5 minutes.
- Cut sweet potatoes in half lengthwise.
- In a small bowl, combine melted butter, honey, and cinnamon.
- Brush mixture onto the sweet potato halves.
- Place sweet potatoes back onto the baking sheet and bake for an additional 5 minutes.
- Remove from oven and serve.

Nutrients Facts (per serving): Calories: 191 kcal Fat: 6 g Carbohydrates: 33 g Protein: 2 g Fibre: 4 g Sugar: 11 g Sodium: 33 mg

Baked bananas with cinnamon

Preparation Time: 10 minutes

Cooking Time: 40 minutes

Servings: 4

Ingredients:

- 4 firm bananas
- 1 teaspoon of ground cinnamon
- 2 tablespoons of brown sugar
- 2 tablespoons of butter

Directions:

➢ Preheat the oven to 350 degrees.

- Peel and cut each banana in half lengthwise.
- Place the banana halves on a greased baking sheet.
- Sprinkle the cinnamon and brown sugar on top of the banana halves.
- Place the butter in small cubes on top of the banana halves.
- Bake in preheated oven for 25-30 minutes, or until the bananas are soft and the sugar is caramelized.
- Serve warm and enjoy!

Nutrition Facts (per serving): Calories: 170 Total Fat: 5g Saturated Fat: 3g Cholesterol: 10mg Sodium: 50mg Carbohydrates: 29g Fibre: 2g Sugar: 14g Protein: 1g

Yogurt parfait with fresh fruit

Preparation Time: 10 minutes

Cooking Time: 10 minutes

Servings: 4

Ingredients:

- 2 cups plain Greek yogurt
- 2 cups of fresh diced fruit (strawberries, blueberries, kiwis, etc.)
- 1/4 cup granola
- 2 tablespoons of honey
- 1/4 teaspoon of ground cinnamon

Directions:

- In a medium bowl, combine the yogurt, diced fruit, granola, honey and cinnamon. Mix until everything is evenly combined.
- Divide the mixture into four small glass jars or bowls.
- Top each parfait with additional diced fruit and granola, if desired.
- Serve and enjoy!

Nutrient Facts (per serving): Calories: 202 kcal Carbohydrates: 25 g Protein: 11 g Fat: 6 g Fibre: 4 g

Sugar: 17 g

Sugar-free smoothies

Preparation Time: 5 minutes

Cooking Time: 10 minutes

Servings: 2

Ingredients:

- 1 cup frozen fruit (strawberries, blueberries, raspberries, or a combination of all three)
- 1 scoop of sugar-free protein powder
- 1 teaspoon of flaxseed

- 1 teaspoon of chia seeds
- 1 teaspoon of unsweetened cocoa powder
- 1/2 cup of unsweetened almond milk
- 1/2 cup of ice

Directions:

> Place all ingredients in a blender and blend until smooth.
> Pour into glasses and enjoy!

Nutritional Facts (per serving): Calories: 100 kcal
Carbohydrates: 11g Protein: 10g Fat: 4g Fibre: 5g Sugar: 0g

CHAPTER 7 30 DAYS MEAL PLAN

Day 1:
Breakfast: Oatmeal with fresh fruit
Snack: High fibre crackers with peanut butter
Lunch: Baked salmon with vegetables
Dessert: Apple slices with cinnamon
Dinner: Grilled fish with sautéed vegetables

Day 2:
Breakfast: Egg whites with a side of grilled vegetables
Snack: Air-popped popcorn
Lunch: Grilled chicken and mixed greens salad
Dessert: Frozen yoghourt
Dinner: Baked chicken and spinach salad

Day 3:
Breakfast: Scramble tofu with spinach
Snack: Greek yoghourt with berries
Lunch: Quinoa Bowl with Avocado and Chickpeas
Dessert: Baked pears with cinnamon
Dinner: Lentil Soup with Brown Rice

Day 4:
Breakfast: Greek yoghourt with nuts and seeds
Snack: Celery sticks with almond butter
Lunch: Turkey Wraps with Spinach and Hummus
Dessert: Sugar-free pudding

Dinner: Roasted Turkey with Sweet Potatoes

Day 5:
Breakfast: Avocado toast on whole-grain bread
Snack: Edamame
Lunch: Roasted Vegetables and brown rice
Dessert: Baked Apples with raisins and cinnamon
Dinner: Spaghetti Squash with Marinara Sauce

Day 6:
Breakfast: Peanut butter and banana on whole-wheat toast
Snack: Nuts and seeds
Lunch: Baked Sweet Potatoes with Black Beans
Dessert: Angel Food Cake
Dinner: Grilled salad with Shrimp

Day 7:
Breakfast: Low-fat cottage cheese and berries
Snack: Trail mix with dried fruit
Lunch: Vegetable and Bean Soup
Dessert: Sugar-free ice cream
Dinner: Baked Tilapia with Broccoli

Day 8:
Breakfast: Steel Cut Oatmeal with almond milk
Snack: Cottage cheese with fruit
Lunch: Turkey and Cheese Sandwich on Whole Wheat Bread
Dessert: Sugar-free gelatine
Dinner: Stuffed Peppers with Brown Rice

Day 9:
Breakfast: Homemade Vegetable Omelette
Snack: Whole grain toast with avocado
Lunch: Greek yoghourt parfait with berries
Dessert: Baked Sweet Potatoes with cinnamon
Dinner: Vegetable stir-fry

Day 10:
Breakfast: Almond flour pancakes with blueberries
Snack: Cucumber slices with tuna
Lunch: Egg Salad on Whole Wheat Bread
Dessert: Baked bananas with cinnamon
Dinner: Baked Sweet potato fries

Day 11:
Breakfast: Ezekiel toast with peanut butter
Snack: Roasted Chickpeas
Lunch: Broccoli and Cheddar Omelette
Dessert: Yogurt Parfait with fresh fruit
Dinner: Grilled Chicken with Quinoa

Day 12:
Breakfast: Quinoa porridge with cinnamon
Snack: Hard-boiled eggs
Lunch: Chicken and vegetable stir-fry
Dessert: Sugar-free smoothies
Dinner: Chickpea and Butternut Squash Curry

Day 13:
Breakfast: Smoothie with almond milk, spinach, and banana
Snack: Low-fat string cheese
Lunch: Lentil and Kale Stew
Dessert: Apple slices with cinnamon
Dinner: Greek salad with tuna

Day 14:
Breakfast: Oat bran muffins with walnuts
snack: Protein smoothie with almond milk
Lunch: Tuna and White Bean Salad
Dessert: Angel Food Cake
Dinner: Turkey Burger with

Day 15:
Breakfast: Oatmeal with fresh fruit
Snack: High fibre crackers with peanut butter
Lunch: Baked salmon with vegetables
Dessert: Apple slices with cinnamon
Dinner: Grilled fish with sautéed vegetables

Day 16:
Breakfast: Egg whites with a side of grilled vegetables
Snack: Air-popped popcorn
Lunch: Grilled chicken and mixed greens salad
Dessert: Frozen yoghourt
Dinner: Baked chicken and spinach salad

Day 17:
Breakfast: Scramble tofu with spinach
Snack: Greek yoghourt with berries
Lunch: Quinoa Bowl with Avocado and Chickpeas
Dessert: Baked pears with cinnamon
Dinner: Lentil Soup with Brown Rice

Day 18:
Breakfast: Greek yoghourt with nuts and seeds
Snack: Celery sticks with almond butter
Lunch: Turkey Wraps with Spinach and Hummus
Dessert: Sugar-free pudding
Dinner: Roasted Turkey with Sweet Potatoes

Day 19:
Breakfast: Avocado toast on whole-grain bread
Snack: Edamame
Lunch: Roasted Vegetables and brown rice
Dessert: Baked Apples with raisins and cinnamon
Dinner: Spaghetti Squash with Marinara Sauce

Day 20:
Breakfast: Peanut butter and banana on whole-wheat toast
Snack: Nuts and seeds
Lunch: Baked Sweet Potatoes with Black Beans
Dessert: Angel Food Cake
Dinner: Grilled salad with Shrimp

Day 21:
Breakfast: Low-fat cottage cheese and berries
Snack: Trail mix with dried fruit
Lunch: Vegetable and Bean Soup
Dessert: Sugar-free ice cream
Dinner: Baked Tilapia with Broccoli

Day 22:
Breakfast: Steel Cut Oatmeal with almond milk
Snack: Cottage cheese with fruit
Lunch: Turkey and Cheese Sandwich on Whole Wheat Bread
Dessert: Sugar-free gelatine
Dinner: Stuffed Peppers with Brown Rice

Day 23:
Breakfast: Homemade Vegetable Omelette
Snack: Whole grain toast with avocado
Lunch: Greek yoghourt parfait with berries
Dessert: Baked Sweet Potatoes with cinnamon
Dinner: Vegetable stir-fry

Day 24:
Breakfast: Almond flour pancakes with blueberries
Snack: Cucumber slices with tuna
Lunch: Egg Salad on Whole Wheat Bread
Dessert: Baked bananas with cinnamon
Dinner: Baked Sweet potato fries

Day 25:
Breakfast: Ezekiel toast with peanut butter
Snack: Roasted Chickpeas
Lunch: Broccoli and Cheddar Omelette
Dessert: Yogurt Parfait with fresh fruit
Dinner: Grilled Chicken with Quinoa

Day 26:
Breakfast: Quinoa porridge with cinnamon
Snack: Hard-boiled eggs
Lunch: Chicken and vegetable stir-fry
Dessert: Sugar-free smoothies
Dinner: Chickpea and Butternut Squash Curry

Day 27:
Breakfast: Smoothie with almond milk, spinach, and banana
Snack: Low-fat string cheese
Lunch: Lentil and Kale Stew
Dessert: Apple slices with cinnamon
Dinner: Greek salad with tuna

Day 28:
Breakfast: Oat bran muffins with walnuts
snack: Protein smoothie with almond milk
Lunch: Tuna and White Bean Salad
Dessert: Angel Food Cake
Dinner: Turkey Burger with

Day 29:
Breakfast: Almond flour pancakes with blueberries
Snack: Cucumber slices with tuna
Lunch: Egg Salad on Whole Wheat Bread
Dessert: Baked bananas with cinnamon
Dinner: Baked Sweet potato fries

Day 30:
Breakfast: Ezekiel toast with peanut butter
Snack: Roasted Chickpeas
Lunch: Broccoli and Cheddar Omelette
Dessert: Yogurt Parfait with fresh fruit
Dinner: Grilled Chicken with Quinoa

CONCLUSION

In conclusion, Diabetic Cookbook for Teenagers is a great resource that offers comprehensive health solutions for teens living with diabetes. With delicious, easy-to-follow recipes, this cookbook is designed to help teens enjoy food while maintaining a healthy diet and a balanced lifestyle. The book includes a variety of meal ideas that are tailored to the unique needs of people living with diabetes, as well as helpful tips for managing their blood sugar. Furthermore, the cookbook also provides teens and their families with important information on what to eat, how to eat, and how to find support.

Diabetic Cookbook for Teenagers is an invaluable resource for coping with this complicated condition. With its nutritious and flavourful recipes, teens can enjoy food without compromising their health. In addition, the book offers lots of guidance for managing diabetes and a variety of tools to help teens stay motivated and empowered. Overall, this book is a must-have for anyone looking to make positive changes to their diet and lifestyle.

Whether a teen is just starting out on their diabetes journey or has been living with the condition for some time, Diabetic Cookbook for Teenagers is a great resource that can provide them with the support they need. In the end, this cookbook provides teens with the necessary tools to make the right food choices and lead a healthier lifestyle.

With its great recipes, helpful advice, and guidance on managing diabetes, Diabetic Cookbook for Teenagers is a great resource for teens and their parents.

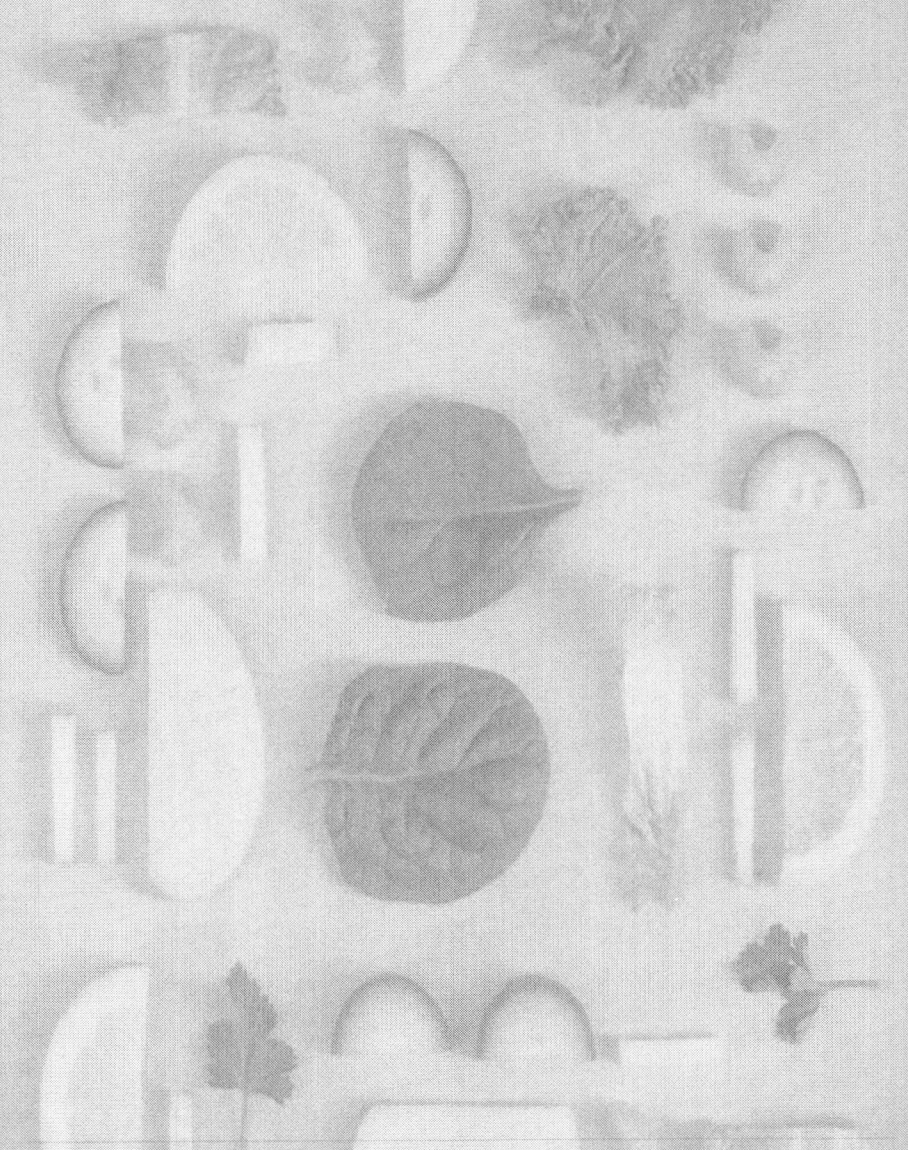

BONUS
10 Exercises

Walking: Walking is a low-impact exercise that can be easily incorporated into a daily routine. Aim for at least 30 minutes of brisk walking most days of the week.

Jogging or running: More intense than walking, jogging or running can help improve cardiovascular fitness and insulin sensitivity. Start gradually and increase intensity over time.

Cycling: Whether on a stationary bike or outdoors, cycling is a great aerobic exercise that is easy on the joints and can be enjoyed by teenagers.

Swimming: Swimming is a low-impact, full-body exercise that can help improve cardiovascular health, muscle strength, and flexibility.

Strength training: Incorporating resistance exercises, such as weightlifting or bodyweight exercises, can help build muscle mass and improve insulin sensitivity. Proper form and supervision are crucial to prevent injury.

Yoga: Practicing yoga can enhance flexibility, strength, and balance, while also promoting relaxation and stress reduction. It may also have positive effects on blood sugar control.

High-intensity interval training (HIIT): HIIT involves short bursts of intense exercise followed by periods of rest. It can be an effective way to improve cardiovascular fitness and insulin sensitivity in less time.

Dancing: Dancing is a fun and engaging way to increase physical activity. Whether it's hip-hop, Zumba, or ballet, dancing can help burn calories and improve overall fitness.

Sports: Encourage teenagers to participate in team sports like soccer, basketball, or tennis, as they provide a combination of aerobic exercise, coordination, and social interaction.

Circuit training: Combining different exercises into a circuit can provide a well-rounded workout. Include a mix of aerobic activities, strength training, and flexibility exercises.

Daily Routine:

Morning Routine:

7:00am - Wake up, drink a glass of lukewarm water with lemon juice

7:30am - Do light exercises like walking, jogging or yoga

8:00am - Have a healthy breakfast containing complex carbs, proteins and healthy fats

9:00am - Monitor blood sugar levels

Mid-day Routine:

12:00pm - Have a healthy lunch with plenty of vegetables and lean proteins

2:00pm - Take a short walk

3:00pm - Snack on unsalted nuts or fruits

4:00pm - Monitor blood sugar levels

Evening Routine:

6:00pm - Have a light dinner with complex carbs, proteins and healthy fats

7:00pm - Take a relaxing bath

8:00pm - Monitor blood sugar levels

9:00pm - Read a book or listen to calming music

10:00pm - Go to bed

Bedtime Routine:

10:30pm - Drink a glass of lukewarm water with lemon juice

11:00pm - Take prescribed medications for diabetes

11:30pm - Meditate or practice deep breathing exercises

WEEKLY MEAL PLANNER

MONDAY	BREAKFAST	
	LUNCH	
	DINNER	
TUESDAY	BREAKFAST	
	LUNCH	
	DINNER	
WEDNESDAY	BREAKFAST	
	LUNCH	
	DINNER	
THURSDAY	BREAKFAST	
	LUNCH	
	DINNER	
FRIDAY	BREAKFAST	
	LUNCH	
	DINNER	
SATURDAY	BREAKFAST	
	LUNCH	
	DINNER	
SUNDAY	BREAKFAST	
	LUNCH	
	DINNER	

GROCERY LIST

SNACKS

Name: _____
Date: _____
Day: _____

FOOD JOURNAL

HUNGER SCALE: 0-10

Time	Food and Beverage /Quality	Previous Activity	Hunger Scale	Mood, thoughts and/or feelings	Binge?	Purge?	Comments
			—10 —9 —8 —7 —6 —5 —4 —3 —2 —1				
			—10 —9 —8 —7 —6 —5 —4 —3 —2 —1				
			—10 —9 —8 —7 —6 —5 —4 —3 —2 —1				
			—10 —9 —8 —7 —6 —5 —4 —3 —2 —1				
			—10 —9 —8 —7 —6 —5 —4 —3 —2 —1				
			—10 —9 —8 —7 —6 —5 —4 —3 —2 —1				
			—10 —9 —8 —7 —6 —5 —4 —3 —2 —1				
			—10 —9 —8 —7 —6 —5 —4 —3 —2 —1				
			—10 —9 —8 —7 —5 —3 —2 —1				

DAILY BLOOD SUGAR
LOG BOOK

DATE AND TIME	BEFORE BREAKFAST	BEFORE LUNCH	BEFORE DINNER	EVENING	OTHERS

DIABETIC MEDICATION: _____

SICK DAY RULES: _____

CONTACT MD WHEN: _____

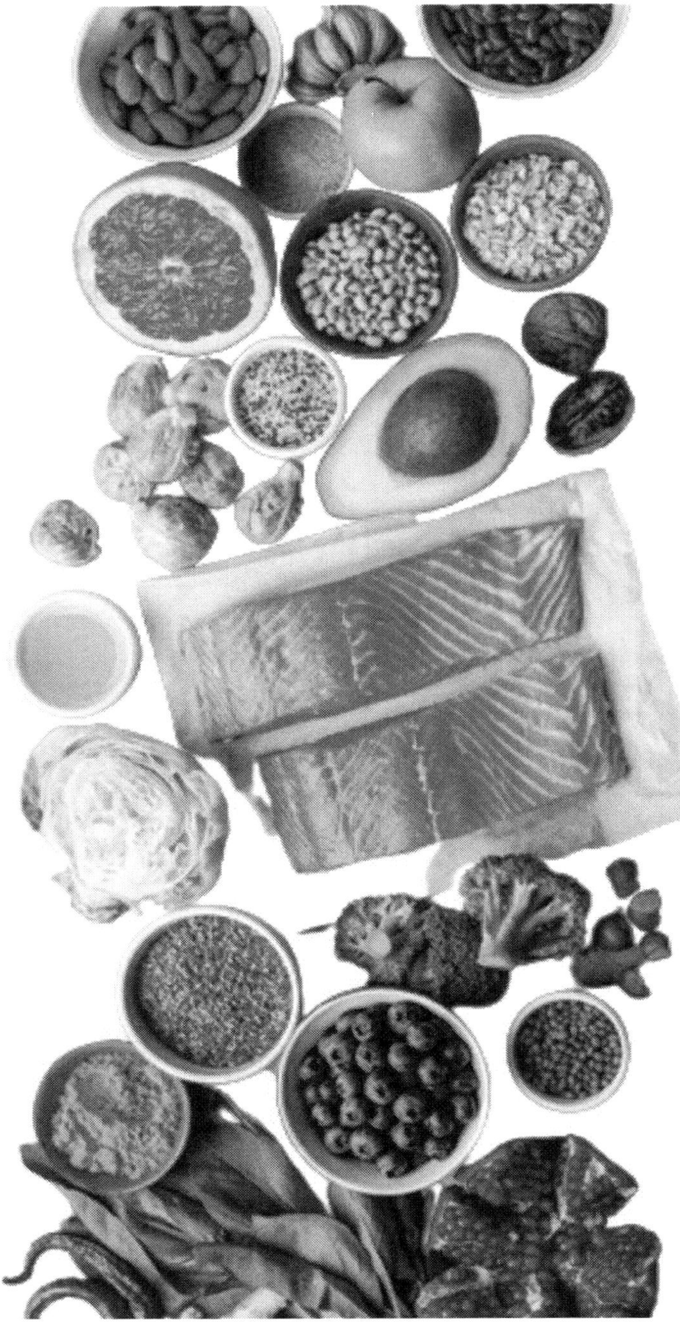